I0569464

DR. JENNIFER FIGUEROA

Thriving Across Cultures

A Practical Handbook for Developing Intercultural Fluency

CASA FIGUEROA
PRESS

First published by Casa Figueroa Press 2025

Disclaimer:

In this book, I utilize story illustrations based on real-life experiences. In order to protect the personal privacy of all individuals, I have adjusted identifying information such as names, gender identities, and specific native countries.

This book is intended for informational and educational purposes only. The author and publisher make no guarantees of any specific results and disclaim liability for any loss or damage allegedly arising from the use of the material contained herein.

First edition

ISBN: 979-8-218-77887-3

This book was professionally typeset on Reedsy.
Find out more at reedsy.com

To the Father, Son, and Holy Spirit—my eternal source, inspiration, and sustainer.

To my mother, steadfast rock and dearest cheerleader, who has reminded me of my worth and calling.

To my family, friends, and the Doctoral Cut Up Crew, whose love, support, and wisdom continually inspire.

And to you, the one reading this book, may these pages not only instruct but transform, guiding you to behold and cherish the beauty of difference.

"Intercultural Fluency is the vehicle through which we effectively navigate difference, bridge cultural divides, and appreciate the diverse beauty all around us. It isn't optional. It's essential."

– Dr. Jennifer Figueroa

Contents

Acknowledgments

Above all, I thank God for His direction, wisdom, sustaining strength, faithfulness, and inspiration throughout this process. May He receive all the glory (Zechariah 4:6; 1 Corinthians 10:31).

Mom, thank you for your steadfast love, unrelenting support, and encouragement. You have built me up, cheered me on, and reminded me who and whose I am. Te amo mucho.

To my family and friends, thank you for every late-night phone call, every prayer, every encouraging word, every thoughtful text, every listening ear, every tear shared, and every celebration. I am so grateful to be surrounded by a community of love, support, and safety.

Dr. Richardson, your coaching, guidance, and unwavering belief in me transformed me into not only a more competent scholar-practitioner but also a stronger, more resilient, and confident person.

Dr. Gary, your heart for raising up the next generation of leaders inspired me to dig deeper and reach farther than I thought possible.

Dr. Roehrman, your academic rigor and encouragement drew out the best in each of us, shaping our commitment to excellence and preparing us for the road ahead.

To the leaders and learners I have had the privilege to work with over the years, thank you for trusting me with your stories and your growth. Your courage and vulnerability have been foundational to this work and have enriched my own journey immeasurably.

And finally, to you, the reader, thank you for picking up this book and leaning into the process. May it guide you to connect more deeply with the world and the people in it, and may it inspire you to thrive across cultures.

With heartfelt gratitude,
   Dr. Jennifer Figueroa

About the Author

Dr. Jennifer L. Figueroa is a leadership coach, Intercultural Fluency expert, and founder of Eudaimonia Professional Coaching. With a doctorate in Strategic Leadership and a concentration in Leadership Coaching, she helps leaders and organizations develop Intercultural Fluency through Cultural Intelligence, awareness, and adaptive communication skills. Her work supports professionals to thrive both interculturally and in creating collaborative organizational cultures that foster high performance. Through practical coaching and reflective practices, Dr. Figueroa empowers clients and readers to thrive across cultures and lead with confidence.

Preface

A Personal Welcome

Welcome and congratulations on taking the first step towards thriving across cultures! If you have picked up this book, it likely means you are curious about culture, eager to connect across differences, or ready to grow in your ability to navigate intercultural spaces confidently.

I assure you right away: you are in the right place. This book is not a textbook full of abstract theories, nor a step-by-step manual that only works in certain countries or organizations. Instead, it is a practical, accessible guide designed to help you explore, understand, and leverage culture as a superpower both in your professional life and in your personal relationships.

Think of this as a personal invitation to a journey where curiosity, empathy, and connection will guide you toward Intercultural Fluency and meaningful engagement with the world around you.

Why I Wrote This Book

My passion for effectively bridging cultures and equipping others to do the same has been a driving force throughout my career and research. This passion motivated me to dedicate my doctoral research to creating a universally applicable, practical model for developing the skills needed to build Intercultural Fluency.

I did not want to simply compile a list of skills to build or offer a theoretical framework that would never cross over from theory to practice. My desire is to provide people with a simple tool they can use for the rest of their lives to grow wherever they are and better connect with the world around them.

Drawing on robust academic research in global leadership, intercultural coaching, sociology, psychology, and intercultural studies, I have synthesized an academically rigorous model, grounded in theory and designed to be practical, repeatable, and comprehensive. Whether starting from a basic understanding of culture or already having experience engaging across differences, this book provides a model to develop Intercultural Fluency and continue building it throughout your life.

Who This Book Is For

This book is for anyone seeking to grow their capacity to navigate cultural differences successfully. Whether you are a professional working with international clients, an executive leading an intercultural team, a student preparing to study abroad, or simply curious about connecting more deeply with people from diverse backgrounds, this book is for you. It is designed to meet you wherever you are in your intercultural journey and provide tools, insights, and strategies to help you thrive across cultures.

What You Will Gain

Through this book, you will develop the foundations, skills, and understanding needed to engage across cultures with confidence and respect. You will explore key cultural concepts, including Cultural Intelligence, cultural dimensions, global mindset development, and cultural competencies. More importantly, you will gain practical tools to translate this understanding into action—building meaningful connections, resolving misunderstandings, and leveraging cultural diversity for personal, professional, and organizational growth.

How to Use This Book

This book is structured to guide you from foundational concepts to practical application. Each chapter is designed to provide clarity, real-world examples, and reflection questions (Thriving Thinking Questions) to help you internalize and practice the principles of Intercultural Fluency.

You are encouraged to read sequentially, reflect on your experiences, and apply the concepts in everyday interactions. The model presented in this book will serve as a guide to construct your own personalized development plan, helping you intentionally grow your Intercultural Fluency over time.

Privacy Disclaimer

This book includes illustrations drawn from real-life experiences. To respect and protect the privacy of those involved, identifying details (such as names, genders, and countries of origin) have been altered.

I

Part One: Foundations of Intercultural Fluency

Stepping Into Intercultural Fluency

1

Setting the Stage for Intercultural Fluency

Where Your Journey Begins

Introduction to Part One

The world around us is more connected than ever before. We encounter people from different cultures in business, education, travel, and even our neighborhoods. Yet, connecting across these differences is not always easy. Misunderstandings, miscommunication, and unintended offense can occur even with good intentions. This is where Intercultural Fluency becomes a superpower: the ability to navigate cultural differences with confidence, adaptability, and respect.

In part one, we'll lay the foundation for understanding what Intercultural Fluency truly is, why it matters, and how developing it can transform both your professional and personal interactions. You will begin to see culture not as a problem or obstacle, but as a rich opportunity for connection, innovation, and growth. By the end of this chapter, you will understand the essential mindset, approach, and awareness needed to engage successfully across cultures and be ready to take the first steps on your Intercultural Fluency journey.

* * *

The Power of Connection: How Culture Shapes Every Interaction

Marcus walked confidently and excitedly down the hallway leading to the conference room. He had just been promoted to a leadership position and was heading to his first meeting as an emerging leader. Armed with his slides, confidence, and expertise, he was sure he would secure this international partnership for his company. This meeting felt like a significant step in his career.

His director shared how vital this partnership would be for the company and that Marcus was strategically chosen to present the proposal for a group of executives from the potential partner company headquarters in Asia. He explained that it would expand their reach to a new country they had long sought to enter and could pave the way for additional partnerships. He was honored to have the opportunity to prove his skills and did not take it lightly.

Entering the conference room, Marcus kept his demeanor confident and strong, masking any nerves. The executives from the potential partnership greeted him with bows, which he returned with firm handshakes. Marcus began to present, and everything seemed to flow just as planned, nods continued across the table, and he felt reassured that they agreed.

As Marcus posed questions to the group, there was silence. Thinking that maybe they were not talkative, Marcus pushed through the rest of the presentation with more enthusiasm and reassurance of the benefits this partnership would bring, but something felt like it had shifted. In closing the presentation, there were no questions from the group for him, so he thanked everyone and concluded. Marcus felt certain he had secured the partnership.

All was well until the email arrived.

"Thank you for your time and consideration. Unfortunately, this partnership is not a good fit at this time."

Marcus' stomach dropped. *Where did I go wrong?* He thought.

Later that day, a colleague from the same cultural background who had heard about the meeting came to offer some perspective. She explained that in her culture, the nods signify politeness rather than agreement, the silence was a way to show respect, and they would likely have perceived his rushing through the silence as dismissive or even aggressive. Marcus had tripped on some cultural tripwires without realizing it in his enthusiasm to secure the partnership.

That experience cost the company potential revenue, but more importantly, it taught Marcus and now teaches us that hard work, expertise, and good intentions are not enough in a global context. Without Intercultural Fluency, even our best efforts can falter. And it's not only in high-stakes boardrooms where cultural missteps matter. Even simple daily interactions, a shared meal, a handshake, a casual greeting, carry layers of meaning we often overlook. To thrive across cultures, we need more than curiosity and expertise. We need fluency. Culture is a lens, a language beyond words. It is woven into gestures, silences, and how people show care, respect, and attentive engagement.

Like Marcus, I experienced this firsthand, but instead of in a boardroom, around a dinner table in a distant nation. As I sat down, two children sat at my right and left, excited to welcome me as a guest to their table. Although we did not speak the same language, they taught me so much during that dinner. Sitting at the table full of delicious dishes I had never had, the aroma of spices and herbs filled my nose. Nervous about making mistakes, I waited for everyone to start eating so I could follow their lead, but I noticed no one moved.

As I looked around, all eyes were glued to me with blank stares, and I could feel my anxiety rising as I wondered if I had already done something wrong. The children smiled warmly and gestured for me to eat first. Grabbing my hands and utensils, they helped me fill my plate and showed me how to properly partake in each part of the meal. Excitedly, they pointed to show me where to place each dish on the plate, which were eaten together, and in what order, all without words. Slowly, the anxiety I felt melted away as they took on the role of my cultural teachers, using gentle corrections and gestures to help me follow in their cultural footsteps.

These children did not see me as a nervous foreigner, but as a new friend with whom they were excited to share a part of their world. Little by little, with every bite, every smile, and every laugh, the language barrier seemed to disappear as we found a language without words. By the night's end, I was no longer a house guest but a friend. The cultural barriers that once seemed like a wall between us had turned into bridges that gave us the opportunity to connect.

Whether in a boardroom or at a dinner table across the globe, the lesson is the same: Intercultural Fluency transforms every interaction. It allows us to build bridges, create trust, and connect in ways that go far beyond words. It is the key not only to success in business and leading global teams, but to meaningful human connections in every corner of the world.

As you read this book, my hope is that you will see yourself in these stories, not just in the moments of misstep, but in the moments of growth, understanding, and profound connection. Because thriving across cultures is not just a skill; it is a journey, and it begins the moment we open our hearts to difference and let it shape the way we see, listen, and engage with the world around us.

Where Your Journey Begins: Learning to See Through Culture's Lens

Maybe you have already had an awkward cultural moment, said something well-intentioned that landed wrong, or misread someone's silence as disinterest when it was actually respect. Perhaps you noticed yourself reflecting on another culture's habits, thinking, "That's not right," only to realize later that your perspective was just one way of seeing the world. This book begins in that space at the intersection of curiosity, humility, and the willingness to learn from experience.

Setting Expectations: Your Role in this Journey

Before we dive in, it's important to outline what you can expect from this book and what will be expected of you. Exploring these expectations first can help you better navigate the contents of this book with more confidence and understanding. Complete honesty and vulnerability are essential not just in this book, but also in any personal growth journey. Developing Intercultural Fluency starts with understanding your current reality: your assumptions, biases, and behaviors.

Uncovering these throughout the journey may feel uncomfortable at times, but I encourage you not to respond with what *should* be, but rather, what *actually* is. You are not expected to give a "right" answer as you reflect, but to give an accurate one that aligns with your current reality. Only by acknowledging these can you clearly identify areas for development and chart a meaningful path forward. This journey requires reflection, self-awareness, and a willingness to engage with discomfort and uncertainty as opportunities for growth.

Engaging Fully: What's Expected of You

Throughout this book, reflection questions are provided to guide your insights and learning (called Thriving Thinking Questions). For example, a Thriving Thinking Question might ask you to notice moments when your assumptions about another culture influenced your behavior. As previously mentioned, thoughtful engagement is essential; the more openly and honestly you explore your thoughts, feelings, and behaviors, the more you will gain. As Passmore (2021) notes, actual development occurs through "the exploration of the cultural influence on thoughts, feelings, and behaviors."[1]

Some discoveries may feel uncomfortable, surprising, or even unsettling. Be brave. Be honest. Lay everything out plainly: the good, the bad, and the messy. Growth cannot occur where awareness is lacking, and self-compassion is absent. Be kind to yourself along the way.

I have never met anyone who does not have room to grow in Intercultural Fluency, *myself included.* Identifying areas where growth is needed does not make you a bad person; it makes you *human.* Use these insights to fuel change and as a call to empathy for others navigating similar challenges.

It is also expected that you refrain from judgment as you explore culture. Avoid labeling differences as "right" or "wrong," "better" or "worse." To illustrate, consider how values such as punctuality vary across cultures. One culture may highly value punctuality, but another may emphasize it less. Passing judgment closes the door to understanding and appreciation. Instead, focus on observing differences, noting insights in the reflection spaces provided, and using these as reference points for further learning.

---

[1] (Passmore, 2021, p. 215).

Your Path Through this Book: What You Can Expect

As you move through this book, you will set the pace for your learning, balancing reflection with daily life and responsibilities. Think of this text as a safe place to experiment, explore, and grow.

Breaks are normal. At times, you may need to pause and reconnect with the familiar to ground yourself before returning to deeper exploration.[2] This pause is not avoidance; it is part of a thoughtful, sustainable learning process. Give yourself grace along the way. When needed, pause, recharge, and return ready to continue your journey.

You can also expect practical knowledge and skills that you can immediately apply in intercultural interactions. And, while it may sound cliche, enjoy the journey! The world is beautifully diverse, and this book is an invitation to begin seeing and engaging with that beauty in new ways. Now that you understand how to pace your learning and reflect safely, let's explore how to shift your mindset and transform awareness into action.

Reframing Culture: Seeing Opportunities, Not Obstacles

The perspective you bring to culture shapes how effectively you learn from it. Often, culture is framed as a problem to be solved, an obstacle to address, or an issue to manage. This perspective can limit growth, as it frames intercultural encounters and cultural complexities as things to "fix" rather than opportunities to understand and connect.

Instead, think of culture like a language, both informational and skill-based. Information must be learned; skills must be practiced. Have you ever tried to learn a new language? Taken a second language course in

---

[2] (Passmore, 2021, p. 221).

9

school or college? The process can feel humbling, long, and challenging at times. In learning a new language, you must learn a new set of words, a new alphabet, and, in some cases, even new phonetic sounds.

Just as learning a language involves mastering pronunciation, grammar, and conversation, developing Intercultural Fluency requires learning cultural norms, practicing behaviors that foster understanding and connection, and mastering your mindset. Approaching culture in this way primes you for effective engagement, balancing knowledge acquisition with practical application.

The Shoe Metaphor: Turning Awareness into Action

You may have heard the phrase, "If the shoe fits, wear it." It is typically used to point out alignment with a, usually negative, critique. This statement implies finality and often leaves little room for action beyond acknowledgment. If you find that you align with the critique, you are left without an option, just awareness.

I prefer a different version: "If the shoe fits, kick it off." Instead of simply recognizing areas where you align with a critique, this perspective encourages action, using awareness of your habits or assumptions as a starting point for change. It reminds you that growth is active, not passive, and that awareness without adaptation limits development. If during this process you find that a shoe you do not like fits you, kick it off and change your shoe. Just because a shoe fits does not mean you have to buy it or wear it. Leave it behind, and find a better shoe instead.

* * *

Chapter Summary

This chapter sets the stage for your journey toward Intercultural Fluency. We have explored expectations for you and the learning process, highlighted the importance of honesty, reflection, and openness, and reframed culture as a language to be learned and practiced. The shoe metaphor reminds us that awareness must lead to action. By engaging thoughtfully and intentionally, you prepare to navigate intercultural interactions with curiosity, insight, and sustained growth.

* * *

Thriving Thinking Questions

- Reflect on a recent cultural interaction that felt awkward or challenging. What assumptions or habits influenced your response?
- In what ways are you willing to be honest and vulnerable with yourself as you explore your cultural assumptions and biases?
- How can you "kick off the shoe" in your life, turning awareness of habits or assumptions into intentional action?
- What does a safe space for experimenting and learning look like for you in your daily life, and how can you create more of it?

2

Why Intercultural Fluency Matters

Navigating Culture with Confidence

A Student's Story of Intercultural Connection

As I sat down at my desk ready to start the workday, I planned to call and connect with each of my new students. I organized them by time zone, starting with students in Asia first thing in the morning and working westward throughout the day to ensure I contacted each one at an appropriate time.

Noticing that one of my first calls was to a new student from a country in Asia I was unfamiliar with, I did quick research to see where this culture falls on specific cultural dimensions. He was from a high-power distance culture, meaning there is typically a more formal distance between authority figures and those they were over. Armed with this information, I decided to introduce myself more neutrally as a partner in his academic journey rather than a formal advisor.

Ensuring I used informal, approachable language throughout the call, I intentionally adapted just in case. The call went well, and the student felt comfortable asking questions throughout the conversation. Before ending the call, I affirmed again that he can call me anytime during my office hours or email me anytime with questions or concerns.

About two weeks into his classes, I got a call first thing in the morning. He sounded a bit distressed, confessing that his assignment due that same day would be late. I advised him to email his professor to explain the situation and request an extension. He asked if I could grant the extension, and unfortunately, I could not.

I heard the anxiety rise in his breathing as he continued, "I just don't know if I can do that," he said. Noticing his hesitation, I gently asked curious questions to find its root. "It's just that in my culture, it is not respectful to contact a teacher or authority without them telling you to do so."

There it was. The cultural norm was at the root of his hesitation. Even though I encouraged him that his professor would be open to receiving an email, I sensed he may need additional support.

"Would it be helpful if I started the email with both of you, and you replied to me and the professor?" I offered, and he agreed. The email was sent, and he composed his reply, reading it aloud to me over the phone to ensure the tone was respectful and appropriate. After reassuring him that no changes were needed, he sent the message.

By the next set of classes, he started initiating email messages with professors and copying me. And eventually, he emailed professors directly by himself. That experience serves as a tangible reminder of how vital Intercultural Fluency can be.

I often wonder what would have happened if I had introduced myself more formally, the way I did with other students? Would he have felt comfortable calling me about his coursework at all? Would he not have reached out to anyone and just not turned in his assignment? If he had, the professor could have misinterpreted it as an unresponsive student.

While I do not know what could have or would have been, had I not adapted my approach, the adaptation made space for the student to seek support confidently while maintaining respect for their cultural expectations. Without this active use of Intercultural Fluency, the student may have avoided reaching out, leading to miscommunication and missed opportunities. This experience is just one example highlighting how fluency allows us to bridge cultural gaps, provide support, and prevent misunderstandings.

A Preview of Intercultural Fluency

At its core, Intercultural Fluency is the ability to navigate cultural differences with confidence, adaptability, and respect. It is more than simply knowing about another culture—it is the skill of engaging across cultures in a way that builds trust, fosters understanding, and opens the door to meaningful collaboration.

For now, think of Intercultural Fluency as a kind of "cultural agility" that allows you to thrive in diverse environments. This chapter explores why developing this fluency is essential, both professionally and personally. It sets the foundation for understanding and engaging with culture more deeply.

Why Culture Shapes Everything

Culture shapes nearly every aspect of human life. As Hall (1989) explains, culture is the medium through which personality, self-expression, problem-solving, social organization, and even the design of cities and systems are formed.[3] From how emotions are displayed to how decisions are made, culture influences how we interpret and interact with the world. Intercultural Fluency provides the tools to navigate these differences thoughtfully, ensuring that interactions both across

---

[3] (Hall, 1989, p. 17; Passmore, 2021, pp. 215–216).

cultures and within one's own culture are respectful, effective, and mutually beneficial.

Without Intercultural Fluency: The Risks

The absence of Intercultural Fluency often results in miscommunication, misunderstanding, and tension. Consider a hypothetical interaction between a U.S. American and someone from a Far Eastern culture where direct eye contact is considered rude.[4] A U.S. American might maintain direct eye contact to convey confidence, while the other party may interpret this as disrespectful. Without Intercultural Fluency, both parties risk misjudgment, frustration, and missed opportunities for connection and collaboration.

The complexity of intercultural interactions increases the potential for miscommunication due to differences in "rules and strategies of interaction" as well as "values, norms, and behaviors."[5] Developing Intercultural Fluency helps mitigate these risks, fostering clearer understanding, trust, and more effective collaboration.

Professional Benefits

Globalization has created a pressing demand for leaders, teams, and individuals equipped to navigate cultural diversity. The Oxford English Dictionary defines globalization as "the process by which businesses or other organizations develop international influence or start operating on an international scale."[6] Yet, a gap remains: while 76 percent of executives surveyed acknowledge the importance of intercultural

---

[4] (Passmore, 2021, p. 29).

[5] (Cosman, 2021, p. 78; Van Luinen, 2016, p. 39).

[6] (Oxford English Dictionary, n.d.).

competence, only 7 percent believe their organizations are effectively developing it.[7]

Intercultural Fluency allows professionals to leverage the strengths of diverse cultures, creating better collaboration, innovation, and outcomes. As Rosinski (2003) notes, effective use of cultural differences can achieve "more output with a given input" by identifying unique strengths within one's own culture while "mining for treasures in other culture(s)."[8] Professionals who develop these skills position themselves and their organizations for success in increasingly interconnected environments.

Personal Benefits

On a personal level, Intercultural Fluency enriches relationships and broadens perspectives. Advancements in technology, travel, and communication have made intercultural interactions frequent and inevitable. Fluency fosters more profound understanding, empathy, and connection, helping individuals navigate diverse social and community settings with confidence.

By expanding one's interpersonal borders, Intercultural Fluency enlarges not only one's social network but also one's worldview. Whether traveling across cultures or exploring social media, you will interact with other cultures in your personal life. Intercultural Fluency helps cultivate successful intercultural interactions regardless of the context or medium of the interaction.

* * *

---

[7] (Mendenhall et al., 2018, p. 83).

[8] (Rosinski, 2003, p. 40).

Chapter Summary

Intercultural Fluency is a critical skill for both professional and personal life. It is not about fixing, managing, or overcoming culture but learning its language and practicing the skills needed to navigate it effectively. By developing Intercultural Fluency, individuals gain the tools to confidently engage, leverage cultural diversity, and build deeper connections across all areas of life. The benefits, enhanced collaboration, reduced miscommunication, and enriched relationships, underscore why fluency is not optional but essential in today's globalized world.

* * *

Thriving Thinking Questions

- How has a lack of Intercultural Fluency affected your professional or personal relationships? What could have been different?
- Which benefits of Intercultural Fluency (confidence, adaptability, trust-building, etc.) resonate most with your current goals?
- Think about someone from a different cultural background you interact with regularly. How might applying Intercultural Fluency improve your connection with them?
- What steps can you take today to begin leveraging cultural diversity as a strength rather than a challenge?

3

Understanding Culture: Beyond What Meets the Eye

I Just Don't Get it – A Conversation that Changed My Perspective

After a couple of months settling down in a new state, I started working part-time at a local company. The area I had moved to was very diverse, and I was surprised to find that the staff and volunteers did not reflect the community they were in and serving. While working there, I was the only Hispanic person among the staff and volunteers, and the need for Intercultural Fluency development became increasingly apparent.

One day, as I was sitting at the computer working, my supervisor entered the office. Sitting on the other side of the desk, he took a deep breath and asked an interesting question. "I just don't get it." He started. "Maybe you can explain it to me."

"How can I help?" I asked, thinking he would hand me a task or ask me about a project.

"I don't understand why some people make such a big deal out of their cultural background, race, or ethnicity. Why is that?" He asked.

Blinking several times, it took a moment for his statement to register. That was not what I was expecting. Internally, I took a deep breath and searched carefully for the right words. It was clear that he had no ill, malicious, or rude intent, but instead felt comfortable enough with me to ask the questions he otherwise would not have had the opportunity to ask. At that moment, he trusted me with these questions he couldn't ask elsewhere. I wanted to approach the conversation openly, patiently, and without judgment to encourage a safe and honest dialogue.

"That's a good question. The simplest explanation I can think of is that it is a core part of identity. It holds a similar importance as religion, family upbringing, or gender for a person. It influences how someone sees themselves, others, and the world." I shared, carefully observing his body language and my tone to navigate the conversation with sensitivity.

A couple of moments pass as he reflects on what I had said before asking another question. "What about it makes it so important to people? Can you give me an example?" He questions further.

"It's deeply shared between those who are part of the culture and passed down from generation to generation. I can be things like music, food, traditions, and deeply held perspectives that feel central to who a person is." I explained.

He thought again momentarily before replying with another question, "How is that any different from family of origin? In my family, we had certain foods, traditions, and ways of thinking that were taught. Although it shaped that part of my life, I don't consider it an important thing I identify with." Just as I am about to respond, he gets called into a meeting, and just like that, the conversation is over.

If only I knew then what I know today, I would have had much more precise language for culture. Even though my supervisor wasn't entirely sold on culture being an identity factor and wasn't convinced it was any different than one's family of origin, he was both wrong and partially right.

Hear me out. Someone's identity is impacted by various areas, including culture, but not exclusively culture. Even cultural identity can be influenced if a person finds themselves between cultures. For example, suppose there is a family with a Nigerian mother, a Dominican father, and children living in the United States. In that case, multiple cultures at play will shape the children's identity.

The culture that the children will hold is likely to be blended between all three. They will receive Nigerian cultural norms, values, and perspectives from their mother while receiving some Dominican ones from their father. In addition to those, they will carry some cultural norms, values, and perspectives from the United States. The result will most commonly be a blended mix of Nigerian, Dominican, and U.S. held norms, systems, and values influencing the person's cultural identity, although they will likely identify with all three.

In some ways, it is like family systems where things are passed down from generation to generation, but in other ways, it is different. This nuance is what can make culture complex, and it's precisely what we will dive into in this chapter.

Why Defining Culture is Hard

Culture is a concept that touches every aspect of our lives, yet defining it is notoriously complex. Scholars, practitioners, and organizations have approached culture from countless perspectives, each highlighting different dimensions. This diversity in definitions can be both enlightening and confusing.

Some definitions focus on observable behaviors, language, or artifacts, while others emphasize underlying beliefs, assumptions, and values. As you explore Intercultural Fluency, it is essential to see these perspectives not as competing but complementary, each offering unique insight into the multifaceted nature of culture.

Cornerstones of Cultural Exploration: Curiosity, Compassion, Connection

To engage thoughtfully with culture, three foundational principles guide our exploration: curiosity, compassion, and connection. Curiosity encourages genuine inquiry without judgment, fostering openness to learn about differences rather than evaluate them. Compassion allows us to view cultural differences with kindness and appreciation, avoiding assumptions of superiority or inferiority. Finally, connection reminds us that the ultimate goal of understanding culture is to build bridges to relate meaningfully with individuals from diverse backgrounds.

Navigating Terminology (and Why It's Confusing)

One of the challenges in studying culture is the overlapping terminology across fields such as global leadership, psychology, sociology, and professional coaching. Terms like global competencies, cross-cultural capabilities, intercultural competencies, and cultural capabilities are often used interchangeably to describe similar phenomena.

Other terms, such as global mindset, can carry multiple, sometimes conflicting definitions; Wilson (2013) identifies six distinct interpretations in her research.[9] Recognizing these differences helps prevent confusion and supports a more integrated understanding. This book synthesizes these definitions, creating clarity and consistency to guide your Intercultural Fluency journey.

---

[9] (Wilson, 2013, p. 34).

Influential Definitions of Culture

Several seminal definitions provide the foundation for our understanding. Hofstede (1980) describes culture as "the collective programming of the mind which distinguishes the members of one group or category of people from another."[10] The GLOBE Project defines it as "shared motives, values, beliefs, identities, and interpretations or meaning of significant events that result from common experiences of members of collectives and are transmitted across age generations."[11]

Rosinski (2003) simplifies culture as "the set of unique characteristics that distinguishes its members from another group."[12] Together, these perspectives highlight culture's internal and external dimensions, the role of shared experience, and how culture differentiates groups.

Components of Culture: Internal & External

Culture manifests in both internal (invisible) and external (visible) forms. Internally, culture consists of deeply embedded assumptions, values, and patterns of thinking and feeling.[13] These include norms—what is considered appropriate or acceptable values—the ideals shared by a group; and beliefs, which influence behavior and perception.[14] For example, cultural assumptions about time can differ dramatically: in the U.S., time is often treated as a scarce, valuable resource, shaping priorities around efficiency and productivity.[15]

---

[10] (Cox et al., 2024, p. 380).

[11] (Chhokar et al., 2019, p. 3; House & Javidan, 2004, p. 15).

[12] (Rosinski, 2003, p. 20).

[13] (Cox et al., 2024, p. 380).

[14] (Rosinski, 2003, p. 24).

[15] (Rosinski, 2003, p. 26).

Externally, culture is expressed through behaviors, language, symbols, artifacts, and products.[16] Behavior includes actions and etiquette, such as removing shoes before entering a home. Language encompasses words, pronunciation, and culturally specific meanings.[17] Symbols might include flags or religious icons, while artifacts and products cover culturally created objects such as art, architecture, cuisine, and music.

Visualizing Culture: Icebergs and Onions

Visual models help conceptualize culture's layers. The iceberg model distinguishes visible, external aspects from the hidden, internal ones. The tip represents observable elements like behaviors and artifacts, while the submerged portion reflects beliefs, values, and assumptions.[18]

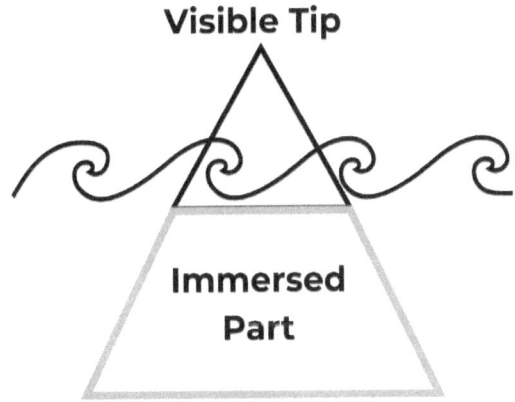

Figure 3.1 – Iceberg Model (adapted from Rosinski 2003).

---

[16] (Rosinski, 2003, p. 20; Cox et al., 2024, p. 380).

[17] (Merriam-Webster, n.d.).

[18] (Rosinski, 2003).

25

The onion model further delineates culture into concentric layers: beliefs and assumptions at the core, norms and values in the middle, and artifacts and products on the outside.[19] These models reinforce the duality of culture, illustrating that much of what shapes interactions is unseen yet profoundly influential.

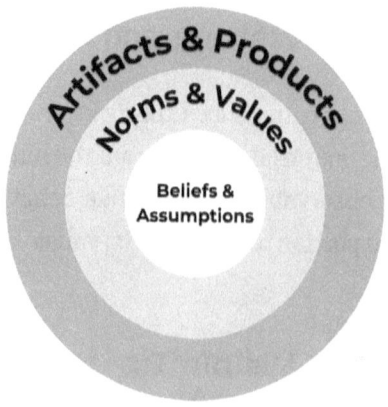

Figure 3.2 – Onion Model (adapted from Rosinski, 2003).

Toward a Clear Definition of Culture

Drawing from these perspectives, we gain a more complete understanding of culture. Culture is so much more than identity, guidance for interaction, and systems by which the world can be understood. We arrive at our definition by synthesizing the distinctive elements from the aforementioned definitions.

Thus, we define culture as a collection of internal and external parameters (including norms, values, beliefs, assumptions, behaviors,

---

[19] (Rosinski, 2003).

26

language, motivations, identities, interpretations of meaning, and significant events) resulting from common experiences shared by a distinct group across age generations, which distinguishes its members from other groups.[20]

* * *

Chapter Summary

Culture is complex, multifaceted, and dynamic. While no single definition captures every nuance, exploring the internal and external dimensions, understanding the plurality and identity factors, and using visual models such as icebergs and onion layers can deepen our understanding. Recognizing culture's influence, both visible and invisible, prepares us to navigate intercultural interactions with insight, empathy, and skill, setting the stage for meaningful Intercultural Fluency development.

* * *

---

[20] (Figueroa, 2025; adapted from Chhokar et al., 2019; Cox et al., 2024; Hofstede, 1980; House & Javidan, 2004; Rosinski, 2003).

Thriving Thinking Questions

- Which aspects of culture (values, beliefs, behaviors, or language) do you notice most in your interactions, and which are harder to see?
- How can curiosity, compassion, and connection guide your approach to understanding cultures different from your own?
- Consider your own culture: what assumptions, values, or norms shape your daily behaviors and decisions?
- How might the iceberg or onion models of culture help you navigate interactions with more awareness of hidden dimensions?

4

Culture as a Superpower: Opportunities and Cautions

How a Cultural Insight Saved the Deal

Mary and her team were responsible for securing international clients for the company. The team focused on both the acquisition and retention of global clients. One day, Mary received a call from her supervisor letting her know she was being sent a client who was imperative for her team to secure. Mary expressed determination and confidence that her team would accomplish the task.

Arranging things with her team, Mary led the project herself so she could work more hands-on and help secure this client. The team worked hard to tailor their presentation and proposals to the client's needs. Each team member was assigned a portion of the presentation to give.

Finally, the day arrives when they will meet with the client. As the meeting began, Mary led as planned, introducing herself and the team before jumping into the presentation. She presented smoothly and thoroughly before passing it off for the next team member to present their section. Team members present one after another, giving their sections with smooth transitions and expertise.

Everything was going perfectly according to plan. The last presenter takes over, Samuel, but before diving into the information for his presentation portion, he takes an unexpected detour. Samuel begins by asking questions of the client and starting a more casual conversation. Mary started feeling anxious since this was not part of the plan. They were so close to finishing the presentation, *'What is he doing?'* She wondered.

She notices that the client's demeanor shifts from reserved and stoic to personable and expressive. Mary watched the conversation unfold with curiosity. Within minutes, Jose switches languages for a moment, and the client joins him. They laugh like old friends, and the client says, "Mrs. Mary, we will work with you on one condition. Samuel leads our project."

"Of course, he will ensure you get the best we have to offer," Mary replies. Samuel shifts the conversation, presenting his section before returning it to Mary to close. The meeting ends, and everyone returns to their desks, but the question still lingers in Mary's mind, so she stops by Samuel's office. She commended him for the great work in helping to secure the client and mentioned that she noticed that he had deviated from the plan, but it worked.

"During the meeting, I noticed that the client and I were both from the same country. In our culture, it is understood that business cannot begin until a personal connection has been established, such as asking about family, background, and things like that." He explained that it is considered rude to jump straight into business and would be interpreted as not caring about the person.

Since the meeting had begun more formally without the personal connection, Samuel perceived the nonverbal communication from their facial expressions and realized that they may have lost interest. In a desire to shift in a positive direction, Samuel adjusted his section to establish a connection. Suddenly, it all made sense.

Mary had missed important cultural cues of which she was completely unaware. She had not stopped to notice that the stoic, reserved demeanor was a sign that things were off. She had not taken a moment to establish a baseline connection to gain insight into the client's usual demeanor to catch when something had shifted. In her eagerness, she dove into statistics, facts, and plans that were not being fully received because of a cultural line she did not see.

Thankfully, Samuel had cultural insight that turned the entire conversation around for the better. Leveraging his cultural knowledge, he course-corrected and effectively built a connection. Mary's experience illustrates how culture can be a superpower and why developing Intercultural Fluency is essential for navigating such opportunities effectively.

Leveraging Culture as a Superpower

Culture is more than a backdrop to our lives. It is a superpower that each person carries, unique to their community and experiences. This superpower is expressed through diverse perspectives, worldviews, values, beliefs, and behaviors, offering a powerful opportunity to enhance creativity, innovation, and problem-solving.

When leveraged intentionally, culture amplifies collaboration, allowing one individual to see possibilities or produce insights that another may miss entirely. As Passmore (2021) notes, the ability to consider multiple cultural perspectives enables us to "come up with new and powerful approaches and solutions."[21] With Intercultural Fluency, this superpower becomes accessible, allowing us to engage meaningfully across cultural boundaries while appreciating the unique strengths that

---

[21] (Passmore, 2021, p. 221).

31

every culture contributes.[22]

Full Definition of Intercultural Fluency

Before examining the pitfalls of cultural engagement, it is essential to define Intercultural Fluency fully. The term 'intercultural' refers to interactions "occurring between or involving two or more cultures," while 'fluent' indicates mastery, ease, and the ability to navigate a skill or language effectively.[23]

Synthesizing these definitions, Intercultural Fluency can be understood as the ability to master both perceptions and interactions occurring between cultures, to communicate easily and accurately across cultural boundaries, and to engage with two or more cultures effectively and successfully.[24] This fluency allows us to harness culture's superpower while avoiding common missteps.

Common Pitfalls to Avoid in Intercultural Engagement

Despite its opportunities, intercultural engagement carries potential pitfalls. One common error is the complete abandonment of one's own culture in favor of another. This approach neglects the strengths, perspectives, and insights that one's own cultural identity brings to interactions. Conversely, some may reject other cultures entirely, favoring only their own norms and values, which limits collaboration and understanding.

A third pitfall occurs when individuals or organizations attempt to create a tertiary culture, distinct from any represented, often mirroring

---

[22] (Passmore, 2021, p. 216).

[23] (Merriam-Webster, n.d.).

[24] (Figueroa, 2025).

their own cultural assumptions while overlooking the strengths of all groups involved. Each of these approaches diminishes the potential richness of intercultural engagement. Recognizing and avoiding these pitfalls is essential for leveraging cultural strengths while maintaining authenticity.

Key Cautions for Effective Cultural Engagement

Intercultural Fluency also requires attention to subtler cautions. Generalizations used for insight can become harmful if misapplied, leading to "unhelpful negative stereotyping."[25] Warning signs include assigning moral judgments to cultural tendencies, substituting assumptions for curiosity, and forming negative associations with observed norms or values.

Additionally, cultural variations are always present: individuals within the same cultural group will express norms and beliefs differently, influenced by family dynamics, mixed cultural heritage, or generational shifts.[26] Because culture is dynamic, tendencies, not absolutes, should guide our understanding. Maintaining curiosity and openness is crucial to adapting successfully and avoiding rigid assumptions.[27]

Every Voice Belongs at the Table

A fundamental principle in intercultural engagement is that every culture and individual deserves a seat at the table. Only by acknowledging and valuing all participants can we maximize the benefits of cultural diversity. Recognizing the strengths of each culture, while remaining

---

[25] (Passmore, 2021, p. 216).

[26] (Passmore, 2021, pp. 216–217).

[27] (Passmore, 2021, p. 216).

mindful of pitfalls and cautions, ensures that intercultural interactions are inclusive, equitable, and productive.

* * *

Chapter Summary

When wielded interculturally, culture is a superpower that can magnify creativity, problem-solving, and collaboration. Intercultural Fluency, the mastery of interactions and perceptions across cultures, allows us to access this power effectively.[28] At the same time, we must be mindful of potential pitfalls, including abandoning one's culture, rejecting other cultures, or imposing a tertiary culture. Cultural tendencies are guides, not absolutes, and individual variation must always be considered. By embracing curiosity, remaining aware of generalizations, and ensuring that all voices are represented, we can harness the full opportunities of culture while avoiding missteps that undermine connection and collaboration.[29]

* * *

---

[28] (Figueroa, 2025).

[29] (Passmore, 2021, pp. 216–217).

Thriving Thinking Questions

- How could you intentionally leverage your own cultural superpower to enhance collaboration, creativity, or problem-solving?
- Reflect on a time when you fell into one of the common pitfalls: abandoning your culture, rejecting another, or imposing a tertiary culture. What did you learn?
- How can you balance honoring your own cultural identity while engaging meaningfully with other cultures?
- What strategies can you implement to ensure all voices and perspectives are represented and valued in group or professional settings?

II

Part Two: Exploring the Framework

Understanding Theory to Build a Practical Model

5

Rethinking Intelligence

Introduction to Part Two

Part Two introduces **Cultural Intelligence (CQ)** as the exploratory framework from which the Intercultural Fluency Developmental Model is formed.

This section is where the foundations from Part I expand into a more structured and research-based framework. While it may feel more detailed and conceptually rich, think of it as the essential toolkit you'll use to anchor your development. I encourage you to move through it at your own pace, underline key ideas, jot notes in the margins, and revisit sections as needed.

One helpful practice is to pause after each chapter and rephrase the concepts in your own words, either by explaining them to a friend/colleague, or even saying them aloud. If you can summarize the ideas clearly, you've truly absorbed them. If not, it's a cue to revisit that section until the insights click.

In Chapters 5–8, we will dive deeply into the research and theory behind Cultural Intelligence, examining foundational topics such as modern theories of intelligence, defining Cultural Intelligence, its four pillars, and the subdimensions that shape how it is currently understood.

In Chapters 9–10, we will build on this foundation by exploring the components and sequence of the **Intercultural Fluency Developmental Model,** a universal, practical model designed to guide your ongoing growth in Intercultural Fluency.

Our exploration begins by asking the core question: *What is Cultural Intelligence?* We will first consider the modern understanding of intelligence, then review the most widely recognized definitions of Cultural Intelligence before synthesizing a comprehensive definition tailored for our work. From there, we will examine the four pillars of CQ and their subdimensions, outlining the essential components that make Cultural Intelligence measurable, actionable, and directly applicable to your ongoing Intercultural Fluency development.

By the end of this section, you will have the groundwork built for Intercultural Fluency development. Understanding the pillars and subdimensions of CQ equips you with the fundamental concepts needed to engage the Intercultural Fluency Developmental Model and prepares you to create your personal Intercultural Fluency Development Plan in Part Three.

* * *

A Quick Reframe Makes All the Difference

A client of mine was freshly appointed to an intercultural team. She was eager to do an excellent job. She started working with me to navigate the transition into this new position and build skills to better support her team's collaboration and performance.

She was a strong leader with excellent interpersonal skills and a superb communicator. These traits served her well in her first week with the team. Being a fast learner, her Intercultural Fluency was being developed quickly. It felt like she had unstoppable momentum. That was until a new hire was sent into her team, Sarah.

Sarah was a bit shy, a hard worker, and skilled at her job. Her work was excellent, and she got along well with everyone, making her a seamless addition to the team. There was just one challenge that my client encountered. Sarah would arrive at work anywhere from 30 minutes to an hour late. My client explained this wasn't an occasional occurrence; it happened daily. Being a new leader for this team, she felt it was important to address, but how she would choose to address it would be crucial.

She expressed how perplexing the situation was for her. Sarah seemed to shine in every other area, except for this one thing. My client went through a list of possibilities, trying to figure out what the challenge was.

"Can I offer another perspective?" I said as she paused. "Yes, please. I have no idea what the problem could be." She replied.

First, I offer her a quick, gentle, and subtle reframe. Thinking of the situation as an observation rather than a problem would help her approach it in a more collaborative light rather than punitive. Then, I offered one of the pivotal practices one can develop in cross-cultural approaches: curiosity. I asked my client, "What would it look like to approach a conversation with Sarah from the place of curiosity?" She brainstormed ideas before solidifying her game plan, leaving our session confident and prepared.

In our following session, I started by asking how the conversation went. Recounting the events of the conversation, she was noticeably more relaxed and at ease than in our previous session. She shared how approaching from a place of curiosity helped keep the conversation light-hearted and tension-free. As my client conversed with Sarah, they realized a cultural misunderstanding was at play.

Sarah explained that in her culture, when someone says 8 am, it is understood that anytime within that hour is when others are expected to show up. So, if one were to say that the event is 8 am, anything before 9 am (8:00 am to 8:59 am) is the expectation. Once Sarah realized the difference in expectation, she adjusted going forward.

If my client were to assume traits or intentions, passing judgments based on her own culture, she would've completely misjudged Sarah. A simple question in a curious posture helped to avoid a potentially tense situation and accomplished the goal. This story illustrates a critical point: what we label as a problem often reflects not a lack of skill but a different way of perceiving and processing the world. So, before we explore the framework of Cultural Intelligence, we need to first rethink what we mean by intelligence.

From IQ to Multiple Intelligences

When you hear the word *intelligence*, what comes to mind? For many, it's IQ and the tests that claim to measure logical or mathematical ability with a single number. For much of the 20th century, psychology reinforced this perspective, treating intelligence as a singular, fixed capacity that drove reasoning and problem-solving.[30]

But intelligence is more complex and much richer than a single score. In the early 1980s, Howard Gardner challenged this traditional view by proposing his theory of multiple intelligences.[31] According to Gardner (1993), intelligence can be understood as "different and autonomous capacities that result in many different ways of knowing, understanding,

---

[30] (Razmjoo, 2008, p. 155).

[31] (Gardner, 1983).

and learning about the world."[32]

Defining Intelligence Beyond Numbers

Merriam-Webster defines intelligence as "the ability to learn or understand or to deal with new or trying situations" or simply "the act of understanding."[33] Gardner (1983), in contrast, described intelligence as "the ability to solve problems and to create a product in several ways."[34] This shift reframed intelligence from something narrowly measured to something dynamically expressed across many domains.

Intelligence as Dynamic and Developable

One of Gardner's most influential contributions was the recognition that "each person has many intelligences and not only one," and that these intelligences vary dynamically "according to personal development and the human environment."[35] Suddenly, rather than intelligence being measured and identified narrowly in one way, this opened up understanding to see the multifaceted expressions of intelligence in various areas of human life.

Not only that, but Gardner's theory also means intelligence is not something you are born with in a fixed amount—it can grow. Gouws (2007) even proposed that using one type of intelligence "can improve and enhance another intelligence."[36] Gardner later emphasized that intelligence can be expressed in **varying degrees** and at **different levels**,

---

[32] (Razmjoo, 2008, p. 155).

[33] (Merriam-Webster, n.d.).

[34] (Gardner, 1983; Yavich & Rotnitsky, 2020, p. 108).

[35] (Gouws, 2007; Yavich & Rotnitsky, 2020, p. 108).

[36] (Gouws, 2007; Yavich & Rotnitsky, 2020, p. 109).

depending on the individual.[37]

Intelligences at Work Together

Intelligences are not isolated. They often overlap and are activated together. For instance, playing the piano is not just about musical intelligence; it also requires kinesthetic intelligence (hand coordination), intrapersonal intelligence (awareness of one's performance), and interpersonal intelligence (if performing with or for others). Yavich and Rotnitsky (2020) noted this very discovery that piano playing "requires the use of not only musical intelligence, but kinetic, intrapersonal, and interpersonal intelligences."[38] In other words, when you engage in one area of intelligence, developing it to improve, it also positively impacts the other connected intelligences.

Expanding the Landscape of Intelligence

Since Gardner's theory emerged, scholars have proposed and recognized additional types of intelligence. Some of the most commonly identified include:

- Verbal-Linguistic Intelligence
- Logical-Mathematical Intelligence
- Visual-Spatial Intelligence
- Musical Intelligence
- Bodily-Kinesthetic Intelligence
- Interpersonal Intelligence
- Intrapersonal Intelligence

---

[37] (Gardner, 1999; Razmjoo, 2008, p. 156).

[38] (Bordei, 2018; Yavich & Rotnitsky, 2020, p. 111).

- Naturalistic Intelligence
- Fluid vs. Crystallized Intelligence
- Emotional Intelligence
- Social Intelligence
- Cultural Intelligence

Why Cultural Intelligence Matters Here

For the purpose of this book, we will focus on Cultural Intelligence (CQ). Like other intelligences, CQ is not static. It is a capability that can be developed, strengthened, and refined. It is connected with different areas and expressions of intelligence. This dynamic nature and connectivity to other areas of intelligence make CQ a potent foundation for the work ahead: building Intercultural Fluency.

* * *

Chapter Summary

In this chapter, we explored the evolution of intelligence, from IQ to Gardner's multiple intelligences, and recognized that intelligence is dynamic, developable, and expressed in many forms. Among these, Cultural Intelligence (CQ) has emerged as a vital dimension for thriving in today's diverse, global contexts. With this foundation in place, we're ready to examine CQ itself: how it is defined, what makes it unique, and why it is central to your journey toward Intercultural Fluency.

* * *

Thriving Thinking Questions

- How does your current understanding of intelligence align with or differ from the traditional IQ perspective?
- Which of Gardner's multiple intelligences do you most identify with, and how might recognizing others' intelligences improve your interactions?
- How can you intentionally develop an intelligence you feel less confident in, and what practical steps could you take?
- How might embracing a dynamic, developable view of intelligence change the way you approach learning and problem-solving in intercultural contexts?

6

What is Cultural Intelligence?

Family Meeting

As an academic advisor, part of my role was to manually enroll students in their classes each term. An important part of this process was to confirm the student's desired major before enrolling. These conversations, although about the same information, varied depending on the student's cultural background.

One day, while calling to confirm a student's major, they immediately switched the audio call to a video one. He asked if I could wait a moment before calling his mother, father, uncle, aunt, and grandparents to the living room. After hearing the family call back and forth, the camera was turned around. This time, my student sat with his entire family, all watching me expectantly. "Ok, we are ready now."

When I asked questions about the student's goals and interests, he looked to his family, and his mother answered, "We are thinking about something in business." During this video call, all the questions were asked by and answered by the family members. At first, I wondered if I had missed something until I considered culture.

In this student's culture, collectivism is more common than individualism. Collectivistic cultures often rely more on the community for major decisions than solely on the individual.

This cultural phenomenon is exactly what unfolded during this call. The decisions were considered and made by the entire family rather than just by him. Here, the family was not overriding his voice, but they ensured he was fully supported by shared resources, encouragement, and wisdom. The entire family was there to ask the right questions, gain information together, weigh out options, and come to a decision, ensuring he never felt alone in the process.

They wanted to be involved in every part of the process to ensure they fully supported him, not just financially, through encouragement, but in every part of the process, even in choosing his major and minor. Knowing how vital the role of community is for him, I took my time and ensured I answered every question thoroughly so they could come to a confident decision and trust that I was there to help and support him in the process, too.

From Multiple Intelligences to CQ

Having established that intelligence is multifaceted, we now turn to a specific form most relevant to navigating today's interconnected world: Cultural Intelligence (CQ).

Early and Ang (2003) define CQ as a multidimensional construct comprised of four interrelated capabilities: Metacognitive CQ, Cognitive CQ, Motivational CQ, and Behavioral CQ.[39] This means that these four separate pillars work together under the umbrella of Cultural Intelligence to support it.

---

[39] (Van Dyne et al., 2012, p. 297).

48

Key Definitions in the Literature

Scholars have defined CQ in slightly different, but overlapping ways. Here are just a few examples:

- "An individual's capability to function and manage effectively in culturally diverse settings...a multidimensional construct targeted at situations involving cross-cultural interactions arising from differences in race, ethnicity, and nationality."[40]
- "The capability of an individual to function effectively in culturally diverse settings."[41]
- "An individual's developed adaptability to other cultures."[42]

Across these, we see recurring elements: **capability, functioning effectively, adaptability, development, and cultural diversity contexts.** Notice that throughout these definitions, there is a common thread of capability, adaptability, and effectiveness in diverse settings.

Framework vs. Construct

A subtle but important distinction in the literature is whether CQ is best understood as a *construct* or a *framework*. Merriam-Webster defines a construct as "a theoretical entity" or "a working hypothesis or concept," whereas a framework is "a basic conceptual structure (as of ideas)."[43]

For our purposes, CQ functions best as a **framework**: a structure for organizing capabilities, not the skill itself. This distinction matters

---

[40] (Keung, 2011, p. 9; Ang et al., 2007, p. 336).

[41] (Van Dyne et al., 2012, p. 295).

[42] (Curran, 2021, p. 38).

[43] (Merriam-Webster, n.d.).

because Intercultural Fluency (the developmental skill) builds upon CQ as its framework.

Synthesized Definition of Cultural Intelligence

Drawing from these sources, I propose the following working definition:

Cultural Intelligence is a multidimensional framework of the capability to effectively function in culturally diverse contexts.[44]

This definition emphasizes its multidimensionality (the four pillars), its nature as a framework, and its focus on effectiveness in intercultural contexts.

* * *

Chapter summary

Cultural Intelligence provides the conceptual framework for intercultural development. Defined by multiple scholars and synthesized here, it can be understood as a multidimensional framework of the capability to effectively function in culturally diverse contexts. Next, we will unpack its four pillars in more depth. Cultural Intelligence gives us the framework, but to bring it to life, we must understand its four pillars: Metacognitive CQ, Cognitive CQ, Motivational CQ, and Behavioral CQ. In the next chapter, we'll explore each in depth.

* * *

---

[44] (Figueroa, 2025).

Thriving Thinking Questions

- Reflect on a recent cross-cultural interaction. Which CQ capabilities (metacognitive, cognitive, motivational, behavioral) were most present or absent?
- How does viewing CQ as a framework rather than a fixed skill shift your perspective on your ability to grow in intercultural contexts?
- In what ways can developing CQ help you navigate challenges in your professional or personal life more effectively?
- What initial steps could you take to begin strengthening one or more pillars of CQ in your daily interactions?

7

The Four Pillars of Cultural Intelligence

'Morning' Delay

It was my first time traveling internationally. Our team of about twelve had traveled to a remote region, and the leaders we were working with told us to be ready for a meeting in the morning. We all got up before sunrise, dressed, ate, and prepared for the meeting. The leaders we worked with arranged transportation for our team.

All of us were waiting for transportation to arrive and take us to the meeting location by 8 am. Ten minutes turned into an hour, then two, then three, and we heard nothing. The team started to become restless, and our team leaders reached out to confirm the meeting time but received no responses. Another hour passes, then two or three hours, and before we knew it, it was 2 pm.

By this point, some of our team had returned to their rooms, pulling out projects to work on, thinking the meeting must have been canceled. Shortly after 2:30 pm, our ride showed up, and we gathered our team to travel to the meeting. As we arrive, the meeting has already started, and our leaders apologize for the delay as the meeting continues.

Everything went well, and there seemed to be no tension, but our entire team was left wondering what had happened that morning that caused the delay. Later on, in private, our leaders ask those who led the meeting about the transportation issue in the morning. They looked puzzled, "Delay? There was a delay?"

Our team leaders explained that we were instructed to be ready for a meeting in the morning, and suddenly, one of the organizers we worked with gave an understanding nod. He explained that in their culture, the words for morning and daytime are synonymous, so when we were told 'morning', it was not our understanding of before noon, but sometime during the daylight hours.

Finally, we understood that what we had encountered was not a delay, but simply a cultural misunderstanding. From then on, our team leaders asked more specific questions about the schedule and agenda to ensure everyone was on the same page. The gentle adjustment of asking additional clarifying questions made the remainder of our time together flow smoothly.

This experience illustrates that cultural misunderstandings often arise not from ill intent, but from differences in how we process, interpret, and act on information. These processes are precisely what the four pillars of Cultural Intelligence help explain and organize.

Foundations for Intercultural Engagement

Now that we have a working understanding of Cultural Intelligence (CQ), we can explore its foundational structure: the four pillars. Cultural intelligence is inherently multidimensional, comprising interrelated capabilities that allow individuals to understand, interpret, and adapt effectively across cultural contexts.

These pillars fall into two broad categories: mental capabilities and behavioral capabilities. Metacognitive CQ, Cognitive CQ, and Motivational

CQ represent the mental domain, encompassing cognitive functioning, awareness, and the drive to engage with cultural differences. Behavioral CQ, by contrast, reflects the ability to act, demonstrating the outward expression of knowledge and motivation through culturally appropriate behaviors.[45] In other words, the pillars of Cultural Intelligence are both internal (represented by the mental capabilities category) and external (represented by the behavioral capabilities).

Metacognitive CQ

Metacognitive CQ refers to the mental processes involved in acquiring, evaluating, and applying cultural knowledge. It emphasizes the awareness and monitoring of one's cognitive processes during intercultural interactions, guiding how individuals plan, interpret, and adjust their understanding of cultural norms.[46]

This pillar includes anticipating intercultural encounters, reflecting on assumptions, and revising mental models to ensure effective engagement with people from different cultures.[47] Essentially, Metacognitive CQ represents the intentional, reflective thinking that shapes how we approach cultural differences, enabling thoughtful preparation and continuous learning in dynamic intercultural contexts.[48]

Planning out questions before a meeting with someone from another culture, reflecting on a past intercultural interaction to adjust your expectations going forward, or building self-awareness to observe how cultural norms and values express themselves in your daily life are all examples of Metacognitive CQ at play. At its core, Metacognitive CQ is

---

[45] (Van Dyne et al., 2012, p. 297).

[46] (Van Dyne et al., 2012, pp. 297–298).

[47] (Skaria & Montayre, 2023, p. 1).

[48] (Mutlu et al., 2024, pp. 319–320).

about application.

Cognitive CQ

Cognitive CQ represents the knowledge component of Cultural Intelligence. It encompasses both general cultural knowledge and context-specific knowledge, allowing individuals to recognize and understand patterns in cultural norms, values, and behaviors. General knowledge provides insight into broad cultural dimensions, such as individualism versus collectivism or high-context versus low-context communication.[49]

Context-specific knowledge offers a detailed understanding of particular cultures, including social structures, traditions, and communication practices within a specific cultural context.[50] Cognitive CQ equips individuals with the mental frameworks needed to interpret cultural cues accurately, fostering informed and adaptive responses in diverse settings.[51]

In action, Cognitive CQ could look like reading through this book, going through the Intercultural Fluency Developmental Program, or asking a friend from a specific region about their culture before traveling there. Cognitive CQ is all about acquiring knowledge.

Motivational CQ

Motivational CQ reflects the drive and willingness to engage in intercultural interactions. It involves both the mental capacity to sustain effort in culturally diverse situations and the confidence to act effectively

---

[49] (Mutlu et al., 2024, p. 320; Skaria & Montayre, 2023, p. 1).

[50] (Mutlu et al., 2024, p. 320; Skaria & Montayre, 2023, p. 1).

[51] (Van Dyne et al., 2012, p. 298).

within them.[52] This pillar incorporates intrinsic interest, or a genuine curiosity and enjoyment in learning about other cultures; extrinsic interest, which is influenced by external incentives such as career advancement or recognition; and self-efficacy, or the confidence in one's ability to adapt successfully across cultural contexts.[53]

Motivational CQ explains why some individuals embrace intercultural challenges with persistence and enthusiasm, while others may hesitate or withdraw. Practically, this pillar is the ongoing driving force behind cultural engagement. It could be the external incentive of a promised promotion, or the internal incentive of wanting to better appreciate a specific culture for your personal development. It all comes down to what drives you to engage and develop interculturally.

Behavioral CQ

Behavioral CQ captures the capacity to translate cultural understanding and motivation into effective action. It encompasses the ability to adjust both verbal and nonverbal behaviors to fit the cultural context, ensuring interactions are appropriate, respectful, and effective.[54] Verbal flexibility might involve modifying word choice, tone, or formality, while nonverbal adaptability includes gestures, posture, eye contact, and vocal tone.

Additionally, Behavioral CQ covers culturally appropriate speech acts, such as requesting, complimenting, or negotiating in ways that align with local norms.[55] This pillar represents the outward expression of CQ, where knowledge and motivation are operationalized and made visible

---

[52] (Van Dyne et al., 2012, p. 298).

[53] (Mutlu et al., 2024, p. 320; Skaria & Montayre, 2023, p. 1).

[54] (Van Dyne et al., 2012, p. 298).

[55] (Mutlu et al., 2024, p. 320; Skaria & Montayre, 2023, p. 1).

to others.

Essentially, Behavioral CQ is all about doing. Whether you are using nonverbal gestures like shaking your head from left to right to signify 'no,' or speaking with a different tone and word choice in one cultural environment than you usually would at home, or reaching out to shake someone's hand to greet them, Behavioral CQ is in your external actions and words.

Synthesized Understanding

Together, these four pillars (metacognitive, cognitive, motivational, and behavioral) provide a comprehensive framework for understanding how Cultural Intelligence functions in practice. Metacognitive and Cognitive CQ establish the mental foundations and applications, Motivational CQ drives engagement, and Behavioral CQ expresses application in real-world contexts. By examining each pillar in depth, we can see how abstract concepts of Cultural Intelligence translate into concrete skills, enabling individuals to navigate intercultural interactions thoughtfully, confidently, and effectively.

* * *

Chapter Summary

In this chapter, we explored the four pillars of Cultural Intelligence. Metacognitive, cognitive, motivational, and behavioral Cultural Intelligence offer a holistic foundation for engaging effectively across cultures. Reflection and knowledge shape our understanding, motivation fuels our persistence, and behavior translates both into respectful action.

Together, these capabilities reveal how Cultural Intelligence moves from concept to practice, enabling thoughtful, confident, and adaptive interactions in diverse contexts.

While the pillars give us a clear structural understanding of CQ, they remain broad categories. To truly see Cultural Intelligence in action, we must examine each pillar's subdimensions. These subdimensions break down the pillars into specific, observable capabilities, offering practical guidance on how to plan, interpret, engage, and act across cultural contexts.

As we move into the subdimensions of these pillars, you will begin to see not just what Cultural Intelligence is, but how you can measure and strengthen it in your own journey toward Intercultural Fluency. If the four pillars are the architecture of Cultural Intelligence, the subdimensions are the blueprints, the detailed plans that show us exactly what Cultural Intelligence looks like in real life. In the next chapter, we'll unpack those details.

* * *

Thriving Thinking Questions

- Which CQ pillar feels most natural to you, and which feels like the most significant stretch? Why?
- How might integrating all four CQ pillars enhance your ability to navigate diverse cultural settings?
- Reflect on a past experience where one of the pillars (motivation, cognition, metacognition, or behavior) could have improved your effectiveness. What would you do differently now?
- What small, practical actions can you take this week to strengthen a pillar of CQ that is less developed in your own practice?

8

The Subdimensions of Cultural Intelligence

The Need for Tools and Practice

It was my very first time visiting India, and I was elated. It was my first time co-leading a team of about a dozen U.S. Americans internationally to support community development projects in India. I was passionate, full of excitement and enthusiasm, and brand new to leading teams across cultures.

In the months of preparation, I learned as much as possible about the communities we would be supporting, the organization, people, cultural norms, and region-specific norms. I did as much research as possible, pulling every resource I could think of and speaking with every native I could network with and anyone who had previously worked with this organization and region.

We landed and were approaching customs for our first cross-cultural interaction in India. When I was asked a question in another language and did not understand, I panicked.

Without thinking, I blurted out what we were there to do **_IN SPANISH_**. You read that right. At customs. In India. I defaulted to speaking Spanish in a desperate, panicked attempt to connect. In that moment, it was like everything was suddenly in slow motion. The customs officers and my team lead slowly turned to me with puzzled confusion on their faces. I was mortified.

In that anxious moment, I defaulted to the only other language tool I had available to try connecting. If only I had known then what I know now. All of my preparation and informational learning left me well-versed in theory, but not in practice.

The pillars and subdimensions of Cultural Intelligence, paired with the Intercultural Fluency Developmental Model, provide more tools in our intercultural tool belt and the practice of how to use them properly. By preparing ourselves with a more robust tool belt with various tools to choose from and knowing how to use them, we can approach intercultural interactions with more confidence.

Moving Deeper into the Framework

The subdimensions provide the finer details of Cultural Intelligence, showing how each pillar is expressed in practice. Think of the pillars as the major structural beams of a house; the subdimensions are the braces, fixtures, and supports that give the house shape and functionality. They make the broad capacities of CQ tangible, observable, and actionable.[56]

Metacognitive CQ Subdimensions

Metacognitive CQ is expressed through three subdimensions: planning, awareness, and checking. Planning involves anticipating intercultural encounters and preparing thoughtfully. For instance, considering which communication styles or cultural norms might shape expectations in a

---

[56] (Van Dyne et al., 2012, p. 296).

61

cross-cultural meeting can be a demonstration of this subdimension.

Awareness refers to being conscious of one's thought processes and assumptions during interactions, allowing for real-time reflection and adjustment. Checking involves revisiting initial impressions after an interaction to test their accuracy and reduce misunderstandings. Together, these subdimensions highlight the intentional mental effort required to plan for, engage in, and reflect on intercultural experiences.[57]

Cognitive CQ Subdimensions

Cognitive CQ includes two key subdimensions: cultural-general knowledge and context-specific knowledge. Cultural-general knowledge involves understanding universal cultural elements, such as how norms, values, and traditions influence behavior across societies.

Context-specific knowledge involves more profound familiarity with particular cultures, including their history, social structures, and communication patterns. For example, it may include knowing the role of hierarchy in Japanese business culture or the importance of hospitality in Middle Eastern societies. These subdimensions provide the mental toolkit needed to recognize patterns and adapt thoughtfully to specific intercultural contexts.[58]

Motivational CQ Subdimensions

Motivational CQ is expressed through intrinsic interest, extrinsic interest, and self-efficacy to adjust. Intrinsic interest reflects a genuine curiosity and enjoyment in learning about other cultures. On the other

---

[57] (Skaria & Montayre, 2023, p. 1).

[58] (Mutlu et al., 2024, p. 320).

hand, extrinsic interest involves external rewards such as professional recognition.

Self-efficacy to adjust refers to a person's confidence in their ability to adapt effectively across cultural settings. Together, these subdimensions explain why some individuals approach intercultural challenges with energy and persistence, while others hesitate.[59]

Behavioral CQ Subdimensions

Behavioral CQ comes to life through verbal behavior, nonverbal behavior, and speech acts. Verbal behavior involves adjusting language, tone, or formality to fit the cultural context. Nonverbal behavior encompasses gestures, posture, eye contact, and vocal tone.

Speech acts include culturally appropriate ways of requesting, complimenting, or resolving conflict. Behavioral CQ is often the most visible dimension of Cultural Intelligence, translating internal knowledge and motivation into observable action.[60]

Why Subdimensions Matter

Subdimensions make Cultural Intelligence actionable. They allow individuals to target specific skills for development, turning abstract aspirations like "improving Motivational CQ" into concrete, measurable goals such as building self-efficacy for navigating unfamiliar cultural settings. By focusing on these subdimensions, pinpointing areas for growth, individuals can advance their Intercultural Fluency intentionally and meaningfully.

---

[59] (Van Dyne et al., 2012, p. 298).

[60] (Mutlu et al., 2024, p. 320; Skaria & Montayre, 2023, p. 1).

* * *

Chapter Summary

In these chapters, we explored the four pillars of Cultural Intelligence (metacognitive, cognitive, motivational, and behavioral) and their corresponding subdimensions. Together, these concepts provide a robust, actionable framework for understanding and developing CQ, offering both the mental foundations and practical expressions necessary to navigate intercultural interactions effectively. The next chapters will build on this framework, connecting CQ to broader developmental pathways and practical strategies for enhancing Intercultural Fluency.

Through these subdimensions, you can move from abstract information to real-life examples of what it looks like to thrive across cultures. With this foundation, you're ready to explore how to embed CQ into daily practice, building a road map for lifelong intercultural growth through the Intercultural Fluency Developmental Model.

* * *

Thriving Thinking Questions

- Which subdimension of CQ do you find easiest to demonstrate, and which requires the most intentional practice?
- How can targeting specific subdimensions (e.g., planning, intrinsic motivation, verbal behavior) make your intercultural growth more actionable?
- Reflect on a recent intercultural experience: which subdimensions were in play, and how did they affect the outcome?
- What strategies can you implement to strengthen a particular subdimension in your next intercultural interaction?

9

From Framework to Developmental Model

Moving from Understanding to Practice

Development is an Ongoing Process

In early 2023, I was preparing a residency presentation on utilizing cultural dimensions as an informational tool to help leaders adapt in different cultural settings. Gathering as much information as possible, I utilized the Country Comparison Tool by The Culture Factor Group (formerly known as Hofstede Cultural Insights). The presentation was a success, and I continued with my program.

By late 2024, while creating the Intercultural Fluency Development Program for my doctoral program, I revisited this same tool for the cultural dimensions section of the program. This time, everything had changed. The brand name and colors had changed, the tool now included an additional cultural dimension, and the scores for the countries I utilized were different. In just a year, so much had changed.

This is precisely why it is crucial that we do not ever rest in our cultural knowledge, but rather continue Intercultural Fluency development as a lifelong learning process. Culture is dynamic and ever-changing.

Without ongoing growth and adaptation, we risk relying on outdated generalizations. The Culture Factor Group understood that and was willing to adapt its research and brand to align with the dynamic nature of culture in real-time.

This dynamic nature of culture is why the Intercultural Fluency Developmental Model is a recurring cycle rather than linear stages of development. It is designed to support the ongoing, lifelong process of Intercultural Fluency development. Knowledge alone is never enough. Theories alone cannot produce fluency, but regular practice and adjustment, transforming theory into practice, can. In this chapter, we will do exactly that, moving from the exploratory framework of Cultural Intelligence to the practical Intercultural Fluency Developmental Model.

Why Move Beyond a Framework?

Up to this point, we have explored Cultural Intelligence (CQ) primarily as a conceptual framework, a structure for understanding the key pillars and their subdimensions. While frameworks provide clarity and organization, they do not inherently offer guidance for action. For professionals seeking to navigate real-world intercultural interactions, the pressing question is: How do we develop Intercultural Fluency? A framework organizes knowledge; a developmental model provides a pathway for growth, translating theory into actionable steps. This transition is pivotal for your development.

Cultural Intelligence as a Foundational Lens

Research demonstrates strong correlations between high CQ and the ability to recognize others' cultural preferences, adjust behavior during interactions, and revise mental models afterward.[61] This makes CQ not just a descriptive framework but a predictive foundation for successful intercultural engagement.

Its four pillars capture the nuance, variation, and interrelated nature of cultural phenomena, synthesizing previously disconnected views into a coherent understanding of capabilities and competencies. By providing an interrelated framework that accounts for both internal and external dimensions of intercultural behavior, CQ lays the groundwork for a developmental approach that is both practical and research-based.

From Framework to Practice

The transition from framework to developmental model requires attention to two key design principles.[62] First, non-linearity is essential because both culture and human development are dynamic; individuals never fully "arrive" at Intercultural Fluency. Development is ongoing, with each interaction offering new learning opportunities.

Second, customizability ensures the model can be applied across contexts, experiences, and individual starting points. These features allow the developmental model to serve as a universal, versatile, lifelong guide rather than a rigid, one-time sequence.

The Sequence of Development

The four CQ pillars are often presented sequentially as Metacognitive CQ, Cognitive CQ, Motivational CQ, and Behavioral CQ. However, our developmental approach requires a reevaluation of their logical order.

Metacognitive CQ, reflecting on one's assumptions and adjusting

---

[61] (Brislin et al., 2006; Skaria & Montayre, 2023, p. 1).

[62] (Mendenhall et al., 2013, p. 438).

mental models, does not make sense at the forefront. Reflection and adjustments cannot occur before the information is acquired and interactions have occurred. Therefore, to gain the knowledge necessary for application and reflection, Cognitive CQ would need to precede Metacognitive CQ and Behavioral CQ.

Therefore, a more practical sequence begins with **Cognitive CQ**, the acquisition of cultural knowledge, followed by **Metacognitive CQ**, where this knowledge is adapted and applied thoughtfully. **Behavioral CQ** comes next, representing the actual intercultural interactions where knowledge and reflection are expressed in action. Finally, reflection loops back into Metacognitive CQ, allowing one to evaluate the effectiveness of actions and identify areas for further learning.

Where does Motivational CQ fit in this sequence? Motivation drives the desire to acquire information, apply it, and act, helping to solidify our new sequence. It fuels engagement, inspiring individuals to pursue intercultural learning while sustaining effort throughout the process. In other words, motivation is not just the starting point; it actively energizes each stage of development.

In practice, our revised sequence looks like this:

1. **Motivational CQ** – fuels curiosity, engagement, and persistence.
2. **Cognitive CQ** – acquires the knowledge necessary to understand cultures.
3. **Metacognitive CQ** – adapts and applies knowledge through reflection and planning.
4. **Behavioral CQ** – translates knowledge and reflection into effective action.

Because motivation continually sustains engagement, this sequence is **cyclical rather than linear**. Each stage feeds into the next, with reflection informing future learning, and motivation energizing on-

69

going development. Intercultural Fluency is not a destination but a continual cycle of learning, adapting, acting, and reflecting, ever evolving alongside our experiences and cultural contexts.

The Intercultural Fluency Developmental Model

Building on this sequence, we identify five core elements representing the developmental process: **Motivation, Learn, Adapt, Immerse, and Reflect**. From these five core elements, the Intercultural Fluency Developmental Model was born.

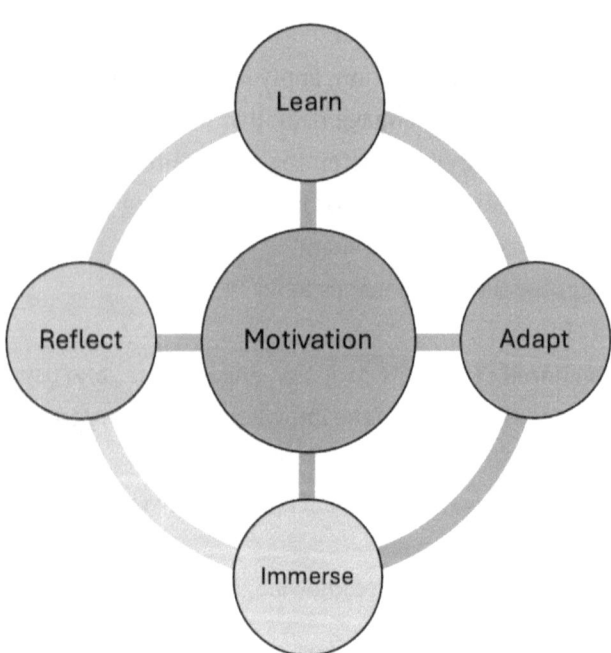

Figure 9.1 The Intercultural Fluency Developmental Model (Figueroa, 2025).

- **Motivation** sits at the center, as it energizes the entire process. It draws directly from Motivational CQ, emphasizing the desire and confidence to engage in intercultural experiences.
- **Learn** captures the acquisition of cultural knowledge, derived from Cognitive CQ, encompassing understanding of norms, practices, and context-specific insights.[63]
- **Adapt** reflects the metacognitive process of applying knowledge to adjust one's approach and mindset toward cultural differences, fostering awareness of both one's own assumptions and the cultural contexts of others.
- **Immerse** emphasizes practical engagement, translating adaptations into action by interacting within intercultural settings and refining behaviors through real-world experience.
- **Reflect** allows for post-interaction evaluation, drawing on Metacognitive CQ's "checking" subdimension, providing space to assess strengths, identify growth opportunities, and refine future approaches.[64]

Why a Cyclical Model?

Unlike traditional linear models that imply a finite endpoint, Intercultural Fluency is a lifelong process. The cyclical nature of the model mirrors the ongoing refinement of skills, knowledge, and behaviors. Each stage (Learn, Adapt, Immerse, Reflect) is iterative, with motivation sustaining the process continuously.

This approach acknowledges that Cultural Intelligence is dynamic, shaped by evolving cultural contexts and individual experiences. The cyclical model not only accommodates this complexity but also encour-

---

[63] (Van Dyne et al., 2012, p. 298; Mutlu et al., 2024, p. 320).

[64] (Van Dyne et al., 2012, p. 296).

ages continual engagement, adaptation, and learning.

* * *

Chapter Summary

By moving from framework to developmental model, we gain both conceptual clarity and a practical pathway for growth. The Intercultural Fluency Developmental Model translates the pillars of Cultural Intelligence (CQ) into a cyclical process: **Motivation, Learn, Adapt, Immerse, and Reflect**. Each stage builds on the others and is continuously energized by motivation, emphasizing that Intercultural Fluency is an ongoing journey rather than a fixed endpoint.

This model equips you to move beyond understanding CQ conceptually and into **intentional practice,** providing a road map for continual learning, adaptation, and refinement of intercultural skills. As you consider the reflection questions that follow, think about how each element of the model applies to your own experiences and where you might focus your development next.

* * *

Thriving Thinking Questions

- How does shifting from understanding CQ as a framework to applying it as a developmental model change your approach to learning intercultural skills?
- Which element of the model (Motivation, Learn, Adapt, Immerse, Reflect) resonates most with your current growth needs, and why?
- How can recognizing the cyclical, ongoing nature of Intercultural Fluency influence the way you approach development in real life?
- What first steps can you take to engage intentionally in this developmental process, applying the model to your own experiences?

10

The Five Elements of the Developmental Model

Understanding the Core Stages of Intercultural Fluency Development

Tackling Tension

A coworker and I were assigned to work together serving an international client group. After several conversations with the group's leadership, we arranged a virtual meeting with the entire group. This virtual meeting would be our first time meeting the group. To prepare, I researched information for the cultures represented in the group, and we opened the virtual room early with our slides and notes ready to present. This coworker and I had worked together with several client groups before, but never an international one.

As the group signed in, we introduced ourselves, had some banter getting to know everyone, and jumped into our presentation. Everything was going according to plan. That is, until the Q&A part of the meeting.

As my coworker answered questions pertaining to his role and expertise, I noticed a shift in the group. Anytime he addressed someone from their leadership, the group members in reply would be sure to say the leader's name with their title, as if emphasizing it. From this point forward, I adjusted the language in my responses to ensure I included titles when referring to anyone in leadership.

My coworker began describing our typical processes to meet individually with each group member to discuss their personal selections from our organization's services (standard practice for the package their leadership had selected). Suddenly, one of the group members spoke up, notifying us that their leadership would receive all information (emphasizing titles for each leader mentioned), make any individual selections, and present their decisions to the group. The tone was a bit tense, and we could immediately tell that a line had been crossed (albeit unintentionally).

Leaning into his Intercultural Fluency, my coworker responded perfectly to this correction, catching the emphasis and mirroring it, addressing leadership by titles rather than name, and assuring we would be more than happy to make this procedural adjustment. He thanked the group member for speaking up, and the meeting went smoothly from there as the tension slowly dissolved.

Even in the middle of an intercultural interaction, which would be in the immerse stage of the Intercultural Fluency Developmental Model, my coworker demonstrated the importance of awareness and flexibility to properly adjust and apply cultural information in real-time. His Intercultural Fluency afforded the opportunity to transform a tense intercultural interaction into a productive one.

This experience highlighted a critical truth: Intercultural Fluency is not just about knowledge, but about applying motivation, adaptation, and reflection in the moment. To help capture this dynamic process, the Intercultural Fluency Developmental Model provides a five-element cycle for growth.

Introducing the Five Elements

As discussed briefly in the previous chapter, the Intercultural Fluency Developmental Model is built around five interrelated elements that guide individuals through a cyclical growth process. These elements (**Motivation, Learn, Adapt, Immerse, and Reflect**) work together to support continuous development in the skills needed to foster successful intercultural interactions.

Motivation forms the central driving force, while the other four stages (Learn, Adapt, Immerse, and Reflect) operate in an ongoing cycle, allowing individuals to repeatedly acquire knowledge, apply it, practice skills, and evaluate their progress. Together, these elements provide a structured yet flexible approach to building Intercultural Fluency over a lifetime.

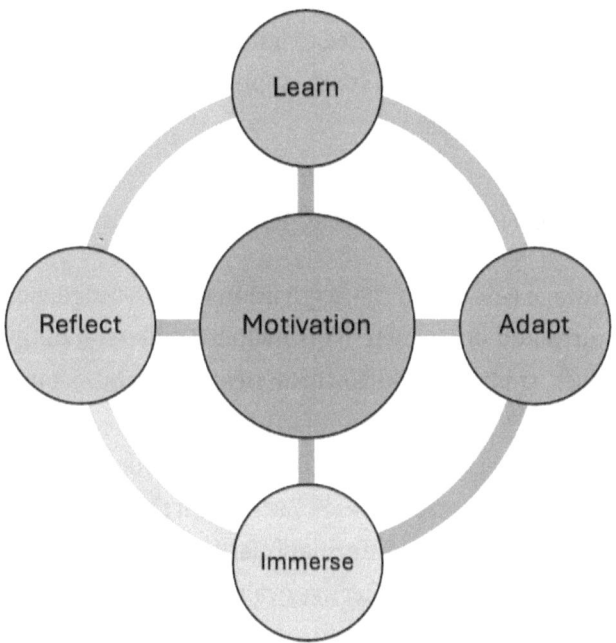

Figure 10.1 The Intercultural Fluency Developmental Model as seen in Chapter 9 (Figueroa, 2025).

Motivation: The Center of the Model

Motivation occupies the heart of the model, powering the developmental cycle. Intercultural engagement requires vulnerability, curiosity, and a willingness to step outside one's comfort zone, often repeatedly and in unfamiliar settings.[65] Without motivation, individuals may disengage when faced with challenges or discomfort.

Motivation, in contrast, sustains effort, encourages persistence,

---

[65] (Rosinski, 2003, p. 36).

and fosters resilience, ensuring that the journey toward Intercultural Fluency continues. It is not limited to initiating the process; motivation influences every subsequent stage, supporting continuous learning, adaptation, and reflection.

Learn: Acquiring Cultural Knowledge

The Learn stage centers on the acquisition of knowledge, both about other cultures and one's own. This includes understanding cultural norms, values, traditions, rituals, lifestyles, and social, economic, and legal structures.[66]

It also involves recognizing how one's own culture shapes assumptions, behaviors, and perspectives.[67] Learning at this stage is not merely theoretical; it provides the informational foundation for adaptation, practical engagement, and reflective evaluation in the next stage.

Adapt: Applying and Adjusting Knowledge

In the Adapt stage, individuals translate knowledge into practical understanding, reshaping their perspectives, beliefs, and approaches to intercultural interactions. This stage builds cultural self-awareness, allowing individuals to recognize the influence of their own cultural assumptions while adjusting their mental models and behavioral strategies to navigate differences effectively.

Adaptation is an active process: it involves experimenting with new approaches, re-calibrating assumptions, and preparing for meaningful intercultural engagement. The more information one acquires and experiences one engages with, the more opportunities one has to refine

---

[66] (Van Dyne et al., 2012, p. 298; Mutlu et al., 2024, p. 320).

[67] (Skaria & Montayre, 2023, p. 1).

mental models and behavioral strategies to better engage interculturally.

Immerse: Practicing in Context

Immersion represents the practical application of learning and adaptation in real-world contexts. Whether engaging with colleagues from diverse backgrounds, collaborating on multicultural teams, or participating in international experiences, the Immerse stage is where theoretical knowledge and adapted strategies are tested and refined.

While traditional immersion might involve fully living in another culture, the Intercultural Fluency Developmental Model frames immersion as intentionally engaging with others in ways that foster connection, curiosity, and the practical exercise of intercultural competencies. This stage emphasizes active participation, bridging cultural gaps, and practicing skills in authentic settings. Immersion is less about geography and more about intentional engagement, whether across the globe or across the hall.

Reflect: Learning from Experience

Reflection closes the cycle by providing space for evaluation and growth. Individuals assess how effectively they navigated cultural differences, employed skills, and applied knowledge during interactions. Reflection can be self-directed or involve feedback from others, such as 360-degree assessments.[68]

The purpose is not self-criticism but the intentional identification of strengths, areas for growth, and strategies for improvement. By reflecting, individuals prepare for subsequent learning, adaptation,

---

[68] (Van Dyne et al., 2012, p. 296).

and immersion cycles, reinforcing the iterative nature of intercultural development.

Why the Cycle Matters

The cyclical structure of the model underscores that Intercultural Fluency is a lifelong journey rather than a finite destination. After reflection, individuals return to learning, applying insights from previous experiences to deepen knowledge, enhance adaptation, and refine behaviors in future interactions.

Motivation remains central throughout, ensuring each stage is approached with engagement, curiosity, and commitment. By following this repeatable cycle, the developmental model provides a structured yet flexible pathway for sustained growth in Intercultural Fluency.

* * *

Chapter Summary

The five elements of the Intercultural Fluency Developmental Model (Motivation, Learn, Adapt, Immerse, and Reflect) offer a coherent framework for translating Cultural Intelligence into actionable development. Motivation energizes and sustains the process, while learning, adaptation, immersion, and reflection provide a repeatable cycle that supports practical skill-building and self-awareness. Taken together, the five elements provide a repeatable pathway for lifelong growth in Intercultural Fluency.

* * *

Thriving Thinking Questions

- Which element of the developmental cycle do you naturally excel at, and which requires the most effort?
- How can integrating motivation with learning, adaptation, immersion, and reflection create a more intentional approach to intercultural growth?
- Reflect on a recent experience where reflection or immersion could have been applied more effectively. What would you do differently now?
- What actionable practices can you adopt to strengthen one stage of the cycle this week?

III

Part Three: Charting Your Intercultural Fluency Journey

From Awareness to Action

11

Fueling Your Growth: Discovering Your Why

Introduction to Part III

At this point, you may feel inspired by new insights but also unsure how to translate them into meaningful change. That's where Part III comes in.

This section marks your transition from theory to practice. Armed with the tools, insights, and frameworks presented so far, you are ready to begin mapping your personal path forward. Every person starts this journey from a unique place, with distinct strengths, challenges, and opportunities.

Rather than prescribing a one-size-fits-all plan, this part of the book will guide you in creating a customized growth plan that aligns with your context, values, and goals. Along the way, you will use both the Intercultural Fluency developmental model, supplementary reflective tools, and questions to help you assess your progress and sustain your motivation over time. Take your time to pause and reflect as you design the path ahead.

Now, let's chart your journey ahead. This is where your journey becomes your own. Together, we'll chart a course that transforms awareness into action, step by step.

* * *

The Power of Motivation

Several years ago, after struggling with maintaining a healthy body weight and experiencing repeated failed attempts at change, I decided to seek the help of an expert. Notebook in hand, I entered her office, expecting a detailed regimen: a new diet, a fresh workout plan, or perhaps a list of supplements. Instead, she leaned across the desk and asked me one simple question:

"Why are you here?"

Her question caught me off guard. I stumbled through answers: "I want to lose weight." "I want to be healthier." Each time, she asked me again: *Why?* After several rounds of probing, the true motivator surfaced. My doctor had warned me that I was in pre-hypertension and would soon require medication unless I made lifestyle changes. I wanted a longer, healthier life, not simply weight loss.

What this expert gave me was not a program but something more powerful: clarity about my **why**. She knew that without uncovering a compelling reason beneath the surface, my motivation would fade, and my efforts would stall.

The same principle applies to Intercultural Fluency. As we saw in the developmental model, motivation is both the natural starting point for growth and the fuel that sustains it in every stage over the long haul. That is why we begin your growth plan with discovering, deepening, and sustaining your why.

Discovering Your Why

Your *why* is your core motivator. It may be internal or external, simple or complex, deeply personal or shaped by your context. What matters is not whether your why looks like someone else's, but whether it connects to something meaningful enough to sustain your commitment.

The process of uncovering your why requires probing questions and honest reflection. Just as my coach guided me to dig beneath the surface, you can ask yourself questions such as:

- Why do I want to develop Intercultural Fluency?
- Why is this important to me?
- What impact could this have on my life, work, relationships, or community?
- And why does that matter?

Pushing yourself beyond the first answer often reveals a deeper and more durable motivator.

Deepening Your Why with Alignment

One powerful way to strengthen your why is to align it with your deeply held values. Williams and Menendez (2023) describe this as finding your "true north," the inner compass that guides your decisions and actions.[69] They remind us that values are the "silent forces" behind much of our behavior, creating energy and sustaining action toward what we consider most important. When your why is rooted in your true north, it becomes more resilient and enduring.

For example, my own why is not simply to have smoother intercultural

---

[69] (Williams and Menendez, 2023, p. 263).

interactions. Beneath that is a deeper value: the conviction that every human being, regardless of culture, ethnicity, identity, age, or gender, has inherent worth and dignity. That value fuels my motivation more powerfully than any external goal.

Your true north will look different from mine. The goal is not to find the "best" why but to discover the one that resonates most deeply with you.

Sustaining Your Why Along the Journey

Like any developmental process, building Intercultural Fluency is not a straight line. There will be moments of progress and setbacks, clarity and confusion, motivation and discouragement. In those valleys, your why will be the source of renewal.

That is why the metaphor of fuel is so fitting. No matter how advanced or efficient a vehicle is, it must eventually be refueled. Likewise, your why provides the fuel to start your journey and the refueling you need to keep going. At times, you may refine or expand your why as your experiences deepen and your values sharpen.

Intercultural Fluency is not a destination but a lifelong journey. And every journey begins and is sustained by a compelling why.

* * *

Chapter Summary

Lasting growth begins with uncovering a compelling why. More than surface goals, your why connects to deeply held values that anchor your commitment and sustain your motivation through challenges. By aligning your why with your true north, you gain a source of energy and resilience that fuels not only the start of your intercultural journey but also the renewal you will need along the way. Just as a vehicle on a long road trip must stop to refuel, we too must regularly return to and deepen our why to keep moving forward.

* * *

Thriving Thinking Questions

- How does Intercultural Fluency enhance collaboration and innovation in your workplace or professional environment?
- Reflect on a time when cultural misunderstandings hindered a professional interaction. How might applying CQ have changed the outcome?
- Which professional relationships could benefit most from your intentional application of Intercultural Fluency?
- What strategies can you implement to consistently practice and reinforce Intercultural Fluency in your work?

12

Locating Yourself: Stages of Intercultural Sensitivity

Knowledge is Power

In my senior year of college, I had been accepted for an international internship program. As we prepared to leave the country, the organization we worked with had each team member take an assessment to identify our strengths and build awareness for smoother collaboration. Up to this point, if asked what my strengths were, I would have mentioned public speaking or teaching, but those were not the strengths this assessment evaluated.

The results were totally different from what I had anticipated. They were connectedness, learner, strategic, developer, and ideation. At that point in my life, I would not have used any of these words when describing my strengths, but as I read through the descriptions for each, I could identify how my behaviors, approach, and perspective aligned with these strengths.

Ultimately, from this assessment onward, I learned not only how to identify these strengths in action but also began practicing how to leverage them in personal and professional settings. The strength of connectedness was most apparent when I imagined all possible outcomes of a given decision or action.

The ideation strength appeared most often in brainstorming meetings, where letting creativity seek out new, innovative ideas brought energy and excitement to my work. The learner strength expresses itself in my lifelong learning and years of ongoing higher education. The strategic strength demonstrates itself more openly in my current professional field, strategic leadership. And the developer strength expresses itself in my coaching and consulting practices as a driving factor in everything I do, desiring to see others thrive to their fullest potential.

This one assessment gave language for strengths I could not even see at the time and supported my ongoing development both professionally and personally. It was a pivotal point in my developmental journey. This is precisely what a supplementary tool does.

It shows us where we are currently, for better or worse, helping us chart the path ahead more effectively. Utilizing supplementary assessments is a crucial part of development. Thus, as you create your personal Intercultural Fluency Development Plan, it is essential to have a diagnostic tool that lets you see exactly where you are today, as well as your strengths and weaknesses, so that you can make a more informed action plan going forward.

Supplementary Diagnostic Tool

As you begin creating your Intercultural Fluency Development Plan, it is vital to have both a **road map and a compass**. The Intercultural Fluency Developmental Model introduced earlier in this book provides the road map, a comprehensive framework for cultivating the mindsets, skills, and habits that support lifelong growth. In addition to this model, there are other tools that can serve as a helpful compass, giving you a sense of where you are starting and how you may progress along the way.

One of the most widely recognized frameworks in intercultural studies is **Milton Bennett's Developmental Model of Intercultural Sensitivity (DMIS)** (1986/1993). This model describes a continuum of six primary stages of intercultural sensitivity, ranging from ethnocentric to ethnorelative orientations. Later scholarship and practice included Rosinski's (2010) suggested seventh stage that emphasizes integration and transformation in intercultural interactions.

The purpose of introducing these stages here is not to replace or compete with the Intercultural Fluency Developmental Model, but rather to **complement it as a supplementary tool.** Where the Intercultural Fluency Developmental Model gives you a practical, applied framework for building fluency, the stages of intercultural sensitivity give you a **diagnostic lens,** a way to identify your starting point, affirm your progress, and reflect on how your attitudes and behaviors may evolve with intentional growth. Much like the strengths assessment gave me language for my strengths, the DMIS can provide language for understanding where one is in their intercultural developmental journey.

It is important to remember that these stages are not rigid steps to be conquered, nor do they represent a once-for-all "final destination." Growth in Intercultural Fluency is dynamic, non-linear, and deeply contextual. However, having language to describe the shifts in perception and orientation that often occur can make your development more tangible and affirming.

As you read through the following descriptions of the seven stages, take time to reflect on which stage most resonates with your current outlook. Depending on the context or culture you engage with, you may also identify with more than one stage. Use these insights as **a mirror, not a measuring stick**, a way to observe where you are and where you feel called to grow.

By combining the road map of the Intercultural Fluency Developmental Model with the compass of Bennett's stages, you equip yourself with two powerful guides: one to chart the way forward and another to affirm your progress along the journey.

Understanding Intercultural Sensitivity

Developing Intercultural Fluency requires not only practical skills but also a growing sensitivity to cultural differences. Milton Bennett (1993) conceptualized intercultural sensitivity as a developmental continuum of six stages, later expanded by Philippe Rosinski (1999, 2003) to include a seventh stage that emphasizes proactively leveraging cultural diversity.[70]

While this framework is not the developmental model used throughout this book, it can serve as a valuable supplementary tool. It provides insights into your current tendencies and perceptions, offering affirmation of where you might be starting on your Intercultural Fluency journey. Recognizing your stage of intercultural sensitivity can also act as a reflective benchmark, helping you notice growth over time and strengthening your personalized growth plan.[71]

The Seven Stages of Intercultural Sensitivity

1. **Denial** – At this stage, individuals may completely ignore or be unaware of cultural differences. Physical or mental separation from cultural diversity characterizes this stage.[72] For example, consider a tourist visiting another country but staying only in a

---

[70] (Bennett, 1993; Rosinski, 1999, 2003).

[71] (Bennett, 1993; Rosinski, 2003; Passmore, 2021, pp. 219–220).

[72] (Bennett, 1993; Rosinski, 2003, p. 30).

resort area with other travelers from their own nation. Because they never engage with the local people or customs, they may conclude that there are not many cultural differences or remain unaware that such differences exist.

2. **Defense** – Cultural differences are recognized but viewed negatively. Individuals may feel a sense of superiority toward their own culture and unfairly critique other cultures.[73] For example, a new employee to a multinational team who notices colleagues doing things differently than they are used to and initially thinks, "Our way of doing things is more efficient."

3. **Minimization** – Differences are acknowledged but trivialized. This stage often manifests as the belief that "we are all the same," overlooking the uniqueness of other cultures.[74] For example, imagine a manager tells their diverse team, "I don't see difference. We are all the same here." Although the intention is to promote unity, they unintentionally overlook how different communication styles, expectations, and holidays may matter to team members.

4. **Acceptance** – Here, cultural differences are genuinely understood and appreciated, not merely intellectually or morally acknowledged, but instinctively and emotionally valued.[75] For example, an individual traveling for work notices how colleagues from another country approach decision-making more communally. Rather than comparing it to their own norm, they appreciate the strength of collaboration within this cultural context.

5. **Adaptation** – Individuals begin to modify their behavior in response to cultural differences, stepping outside their cultural comfort zone. Rosinski emphasizes adaptation over adoption or

---

[73] (Rosinski, 2003, p. 30).

[74] (Rosinski, 2003, p. 30).

[75] (Rosinski, 2003, p. 30; Passmore, 2021, p. 217).

assimilation, meaning that one adjusts approaches while maintaining one's own cultural identity.[76] For example, a team leader adjusting their communication style to use more pauses and indirect phrasing when facilitating with colleagues who prefer high-context communication, without losing their authentic leadership voice.

6. **Integration** – Cultural differences are fully incorporated into one's perspective. Individuals can view and evaluate situations from multiple cultural frames while remaining grounded in their own culture.[77] For example, a bi-cultural professional mediating a conflict, considering both individualistic and collectivistic viewpoints before proposing a solution.

7. **Leveraging Differences** – The seventh stage, added by Rosinski, focuses on proactively seeking opportunities in cultural diversity. This stage emphasizes creating synergy by identifying the unique strengths, "gems," of each culture and leveraging them collectively for greater performance, creativity, and fulfillment.[78] For example, on a global innovation team, combining diverse problem-solving approaches like one person's structured planning with another's improvisational creativity to design a more effective strategy together.

---

[76] (Rosinski, 2003, p. 30; Passmore, 2021, p. 220).

[77] (Rosinski, 2003, p. 30; Passmore, 2021, p. 221).

[78] (Rosinski, 2003, pp. 40–41).

Ethnocentric and Ethnorelative Perspectives

These seven stages can also be grouped into two overarching approaches: **ethnocentric** and **ethnorelative**.

- **Ethnocentric** (Stages 1–3) assumes one's own culture is central to reality, interpreting others through the lens of one's cultural norms, values, and assumptions.[79] For example, punctuality may be highly valued in one culture, leading an individual to interpret a colleague's lateness from another culture as careless or disrespectful.
- **Ethnorelative** (Stages 4–7) acknowledges and values cultural differences without assuming the centrality or superiority of one's own culture. It emphasizes observation, engagement, and adaptation while preserving the integrity of one's own cultural identity.[80]

It is important to recognize that these stages are **non-successive**.[81] Progression is not linear, and one may shift between stages depending on context, experience, and reflection.

Adoption, Assimilation, and Adaptation

Understanding stage five requires clarity about the differences between **adoption, assimilation, and adaptation**. Merriam-Webster defines:

- **Adopt**: "To begin to practice or use."[82]
- **Assimilate**: "To absorb into the cultural tradition of a population

---

[79] (Rosinski, 2003, p. 31).

[80] (Rosinski, 2003, p. 34).

[81] (Rosinski, 2003, p. 30).

[82] (Merriam-Webster, n.d.).

97

or group" or "to make similar."[83]
- **Adapt**: "To make fit (as for a new use), often by modification."[84]

Cultural adaptation involves modifying one's behaviors and approaches to resonate across differences, **without absorbing or replacing one's own cultural identity**. As Passmore (2021) notes, "Empathy does not mean permanently giving up your own cultural identity."[85] Adaptation allows one to engage effectively across cultures while honoring both self and others.

Reflection: Where Are You?

Pause for reflection: consider a recent intercultural interaction. Observe your choices, assumptions, and inner dialogue. Ask yourself:

- Which stage do I fall into?
- Do I approach interactions ethnocentrically or ethnorelatively?

Avoid assigning moral judgment to your observations. The goal is honest self-awareness, not perfection. This reflection helps identify growth opportunities and prepares you to engage intercultural differences with empathy, adaptability, and intentionality.

"Think of a time when a cultural difference caught you off guard. What assumptions did you make? How might someone at the 'acceptance' or 'adaptation' stage have approached the same situation differently?"

---

[83] (Merriam-Webster, n.d.).

[84] (Merriam-Webster, n.d.).

[85] (Passmore, 2021, p. 220).

* * *

Chapter Summary

The seven stages of intercultural sensitivity provide a compass for self-awareness, helping you recognize your current orientation toward cultural difference. Moving from ethnocentric to ethnorelative perspectives highlights the shift from centering one's own culture to valuing and engaging across many. While not a linear path, these stages offer language to describe growth and affirm progress, equipping you to navigate your journey with greater clarity and intentionality. Using this tool, you can identify your current starting point with Intercultural Fluency to properly map out your developmental plan in the chapters ahead.

* * *

Thriving Thinking Questions

- How can Intercultural Fluency improve your personal relationships and social connections?
- Reflect on a personal experience where cultural differences led to miscommunication. How could CQ have influenced the interaction?
- Which daily habits or interactions could serve as opportunities to practice Intercultural Fluency in your personal life?
- What intentional steps can you take to increase empathy, curiosity, and connection across cultural differences at home, in your community, or with friends?

13

Becoming an Interculturally Fluent Person

Seeing, Adapting, and Connecting Across Cultures

The Power of an Unbiased Clarifying Question

A colleague of mine led a multinational Spanish-speaking team. One day, he received an urgent project that his team needed to manage. Upon reviewing and absorbing the information about the project, he divided the project into smaller tasks, which he delegated to his team members.

As he explains the task and overall project, his teammate takes in the information and responds, "I'll start working on that now." When his teammate replied with the word for 'now,' my colleague hesitated. In his cultural background, that word meant 'later.' For his teammate, it meant 'now.'

The word used for 'now' in Spanish can vary depending on the individual's cultural background. Although my colleague heard his teammate say, "I'll start working on that later," the teammate had communicated, "I'll start working on that now."

At this point, my colleague had a couple of options to proceed: ignore it, assume the teammate was not properly prioritizing the task, or gather additional information. Being an interculturally fluent communicator, my colleague leaned into curiosity and asked a clarifying question. "When you use this word, does it mean in this moment for you or at another time?" The teammate replies, "It means at this moment for me," putting my colleague's momentary worry at ease.

This experience serves as a real-life example of what an interculturally fluent person looks like. He utilized skills like openness, curiosity, active listening, cultural knowledge, clarifying questions, and an unbiased, unassuming approach to diffuse a potential cultural misunderstanding before it could escalate.

What Intercultural Fluency Looks Like

One of the most important questions for anyone on the journey toward Intercultural Fluency is: **how do we recognize it in action?** What does it look like when someone embodies Intercultural Fluency in their interactions, decisions, and relationships? Understanding these characteristics not only helps identify fluent behavior in others but also serves as a mirror to reflect on one's own development.

Empathetic Immersion Across Cultures

An interculturally fluent person demonstrates a deep capacity for **empathetic immersion in multiple cultures**. According to Passmore (2021), this involves the ability to view situations from a variety of cultural perspectives and to adjust one's approach in ways that enhance understanding, communication, and connection.[86]

This is more than intellectual understanding; it requires temporarily stepping into another person's worldview to engage with their norms,

---

[86] (Passmore, 2021, p. 221).

values, and assumptions. Empathetic immersion can look like using both communal and individual language and motivators while facilitating a meeting with those from collectivistic and individualistic cultures to engage the different cultural perspectives present.

Legitimizing Multiple Perspectives

Another hallmark of Intercultural Fluency is the ability to **hold multiple cultural perspectives simultaneously** without judgment. Interculturally fluent individuals see each perspective as entirely legitimate, avoiding the trap of viewing one culture as inherently superior or inferior to another.[87] This stance allows them to navigate complexity and ambiguity with openness, creating the space for authentic dialogue and mutual respect.

Legitimizing multiple perspectives looks like sitting at a meeting where one colleague expects quick decisions while another prefers lengthy discussions and seeing both as valid approaches rather than labeling one 'right' or 'wrong.

Maintaining Cultural Integrity

Equally important is the **secure sense of one's own cultural identity**. Interculturally fluent people do not lose their own cultural integrity in the pursuit of understanding or adapting to others. Instead, they maintain their norms, values, and beliefs while effectively engaging with and appreciating the differences of others.[88]

This balance between adaptation and rootedness ensures interactions are both authentic and respectful, allowing for genuine connection

---

[87] (Passmore, 2021, p. 217).

[88] (Passmore, 2021, p. 221).

across cultural divides. Maintaining cultural integrity looks like being able to balance adapting communication style to a more high-context culture without completely losing your voice.

* * *

Chapter Summary

Intercultural Fluency comes alive in the ability to immerse empathetically across cultures, to legitimize multiple perspectives without judgment, and to remain grounded in one's own cultural integrity. These qualities in balance, adaptability, openness, and rootedness, create the conditions for authentic connection and mutual respect. They serve as a living picture of what it means to thrive across cultures with both confidence and humility. As you develop these qualities, you'll find yourself not only navigating differences more smoothly but also building deeper trust, collaboration, and creativity in every intercultural setting.

* * *

Thriving Thinking Questions

- How will you maintain motivation for ongoing intercultural development in the face of setbacks or discomfort?
- Which aspects of the developmental cycle (Motivation, Learn, Adapt, Immerse, Reflect) will require the most attention for your continued growth?
- Reflect on your progress so far: what key insights or habits have contributed most to your Intercultural Fluency?
- What long-term practices can you put in place to ensure your Intercultural Fluency continues to evolve and strengthen over time?

14

Creating Your Intercultural Fluency Development Plan

"A goal without a plan is just a wish."

– Antoine de Saint-Exupéry

The Importance of a Plan

A coaching client I worked with expressed a list of goals he wanted to work on, including career development, going back to school, starting a family, and getting healthy. As we dug further, he mentioned that getting healthy had been something that had "always been a goal," but he simply had not gotten around to it yet.

He reminisced about how great he felt when he used to run two miles daily, but immediately lamented that it would be impossible in his current season of life. Using intentional questions, we explored this lament, and he expressed that his current schedule doesn't allow him to do that. I shared with him that **movement is where a dream transitions**

to a goal and does not always take the form we expect.

He looked at me curiously as I continued. I expressed that we often think of movement or progress as the goal being completed, a significant milestone being perfectly achieved, or returning to a previous routine. In this case, it was running two miles daily. However, **movement or progress is simply taking a step that gets you closer to the goal**.

He identified his starting place as having no intentional exercise in his weekly routines. If the goal is two miles a day, and the starting place is zero miles per day, anything over zero would be progress towards his goal.

At this point, I could see the wheels turning in his mind as hope returned to his face. By the end of our session, he identified the time he did have available and created a plan to move forward, starting with five minutes of walking daily. It seemed small, but as he built consistency, those five minutes turned into thirty, then grew until he reached his final goal. He used the confidence he built during that process to gain momentum and set plans for his other goals.

The quote "a goal without a plan is just a wish" is attributed to Antoine de Saint-Exupéry, and although it seems harsh at first glance, there is truth in it. Creating a plan and identifying those first steps helps us progress towards our goals. Without an actionable plan, we stand still, dreaming of what could be one day. An actionable plan makes today a stepping stone toward one day.

Just as my client's fitness journey required a plan with small, realistic steps, building Intercultural Fluency requires intentional planning and consistent movement forward. Without a plan, it remains only a wish.

Forming A Game Plan

As we approach the final chapters of this book, we've explored the foundations, theory, and practice for Intercultural Fluency. All of this information helps build cognitive understanding and may even fuel excitement for Intercultural Fluency development, but it shouldn't stop here.

My desire in creating this resource was not only to inform and teach about Intercultural Fluency in a conceptual way, but to help you construct your first personal Intercultural Fluency Development Plan. It is crucial that you do not walk away from this book with a series of new facts, a new dream to build Intercultural Fluency, but no actionable game plan to move forward.

Your personal Intercultural Fluency Development Plan is your road map for the path ahead to building Intercultural Fluency. In this chapter, you will be guided through taking the information you've learned throughout this book to create your plan for the pathway ahead.

Know that you are not alone on this journey, and this first plan may adjust over time. In fact, you have taken a significant first step by reading through this book and gaining the information needed to ground your development. As you move forward, armed with information and an actionable plan, your Intercultural Fluency practice begins, and you will build momentum towards your development with every step, no matter how big or small.

If your first plan feels sparse, imperfect, or incomplete, do not worry. The point is not to get it right or create the perfect plan, but to start. Plans evolve as you do.

Let's get started.

Preparing Your Plan

First, you will lay out the preparation for your action plan by choosing how you will keep and store content. Are you a more tactile person who prefers writing things down? Then a notebook or binder with loose-leaf pages would work well for you. Do you not like the idea of having to keep track of a binder or notebook? Then you might do better with a digital plan where content is stored in a notes app on your phone, a document on your tablet, or a folder on your laptop.

However you choose to organize your content, it's important that you choose what works best for you and what will be the path of least resistance for you to continue using. If there is too much resistance, consistency becomes more difficult to maintain, which can threaten your ongoing development. Find what works best for you, and don't be afraid to change it if it stops working.

Write Your Why

Once you've chosen how you will organize content for your personal Intercultural Fluency Development Plan, your next step is to write out your "why" (as discussed in chapter 11). Take your first page, physical or digital, to write out your "why." It can be one or many reasons.

The key is to keep digging and asking yourself why until you find the deepest-rooted reason directly connected to a deeply held value. This ensures that your "why" is potent. When you read it back to yourself, it should inspire, move, and push you toward action. Keeping your why at the forefront of your plan and continued development will support your continued motivation throughout your journey.

Commitment Contract

The next step in creating your personal Intercultural Fluency Development Plan is another potent motivator: the commitment contract. This is a document (whether physical or digital) in which you clearly outline your commitment to the process of developing Intercultural Fluency. Deeply held values will likely also guide the statements you commit to in your journey. This contract has the potential to reorient your mind toward growth.

At the beginning of this book, I outlined some essential expectations as you embarked on your Intercultural Fluency journey for this very reason. Outlining clear expectations helps us orient our minds appropriately before the practice begins. Consider summarizing some of those expectations in your commitment contract. Here are a few guiding questions to start. Additional prompts can be found in the Appendix at the back of this book.

If you are unsure where to start, feel free to use the following questions to guide you:

- How do I want others to feel when they engage with me in culturally diverse contexts?
- What actions can I take to hold myself accountable for my intercultural growth (journaling, reflection, feedback, etc.)?
- How will I keep my learning active beyond this book so that Intercultural Fluency becomes a lifelong practice?
- How will I integrate Intercultural Fluency practices into my daily life (work, relationships, community)?
- What personal values or faith convictions inspire me to live out these commitments with integrity?

Identify Where You Are

When you have successfully outlined your "why" and your commitment contract, it's time to identify your starting point. Where are you today on your Intercultural Fluency journey? There are several ways to identify your starting point; however, your chosen method will also serve as your mirror for reflecting your progress throughout your journey.

A formal assessment has the benefit of providing consistent, tangible results along the way. For this reason, I created a free assessment based on the seven stages of intercultural sensitivity (as outlined in chapter 12), which you can take as many times as needed. A QR code is included for the free assessment in the Appendix section of this book, or you can visit www.eprocoaching.com and select "assessments" under the "resources" tab. Use it to get a baseline and track progress alongside your reflective observations for a more complete picture of your growth.

A less formal way to identify your starting point is to reflect on your most recent intercultural interaction. As you reflect, select qualities throughout the interaction where you could improve. As you continue your journey, you can use the same qualities in your most recent interactions to assess progress.

The Cycle

In the Intercultural Fluency Developmental Model, the outer ring is meant to be repeated as a lifelong developmental process. You will use this outer ring to complete your first plan. The four stages in the outer ring are: Learn, Adapt, Immerse, and Reflect. You will set a step or mini goal for each of these four stages.

Learn

Remember that the Learn stage is all about acquiring informational knowledge. You've done that by reading this very book. Setting mini goals in this stage can include researching questions like what norms, beliefs, behaviors, values, and systems are present in this culture. You could ask a native of that culture or conduct research using tools like The Country Comparison Tool by The Culture Factor Group.

Adapt

Next is the Adapt stage, which is centered on the application and adaptation of the knowledge you have just acquired. An example of this could be asking how these norms, beliefs, behaviors, values, and systems are expressed in personal or professional settings.

Immerse

The Immerse stage is the time to put into practice what you have learned and adapted. In the context of intercultural interaction, you will adopt behaviors that may better resonate with the other person's cultural context. Choose to adopt behaviors and/or communication styles that help you connect well. For example, for more direct cultures, you would want to use more direct language, and for more indirect cultures, you would adopt more indirect language. Think: What behaviors can I adopt that will better resonate with this person's culture within this context (personal or professional)?

Reflect

In the reflect stage, you will revisit the intercultural interaction, using guiding questions to reflect and evaluate your intercultural effectiveness. You may use the following as a guide for a structured reflection:

1. What Worked?

Consider what aspects of your interaction were effective. Did certain behaviors, communication styles, or adaptations help you connect more successfully? Record the strategies that resonated well and the positive outcomes you observed.

Ask yourself: "Which actions or approaches helped build rapport or understanding in this interaction?"

2. What Didn't Work?

Reflect on what could have been improved. Were there moments of misunderstanding, discomfort, or ineffective communication? Take note without judgment; these are opportunities to grow.

Ask yourself: "Which behaviors or assumptions might have hindered effective communication, and why?"

3. What's Next?

Based on your observations, consider how to adjust your approach for future interactions. Set small, specific goals to experiment with new strategies or behaviors.

Ask yourself: "What steps can I take next time to enhance my intercultural effectiveness in similar situations?"

Additional prompts can be found in the Appendix at the back of this book. Keep notes on your guiding prompts and questions for each stage as a template for your continued growth. Also, keep notes on the information and learning you receive throughout the process as you develop. Over time, you'll create a rich record of growth, helping you turn awareness into action and action into sustained Intercultural Fluency.

* * *

Chapter Summary

In this chapter, the focus shifts from knowledge to action, transforming the dream of Intercultural Fluency into a lived practice. Using the story of a coaching client who rediscovered momentum by starting small, the chapter illustrates that progress is not about perfection but consistent movement toward a goal. Readers are reminded that "a goal without a plan is just a wish," and creating a personal Intercultural Fluency Development Plan provides the structure needed to make growth tangible.

The plan begins with preparation: choosing a method to organize learning (physical or digital), clarifying a deeply rooted "why" to sustain motivation, and writing a personal **commitment contract** to anchor values and accountability. Identifying a starting point, through formal assessments or reflective analysis, then sets the baseline for tracking growth.

The chapter concludes by applying the Intercultural Fluency Developmental Model's outer cyclical process of **Learn, Adapt, Immerse, and Reflect.** By setting mini goals in each stage, learners build a sustainable rhythm of growth that turns Intercultural Fluency into a lifelong practice. With each step, no matter how small, momentum builds, transforming awareness into action and action into transformation.

Your plan is more than paper (whether digital or physical), it's **momentum in motion**. A goal without a plan may remain a wish, but with each small step forward, Intercultural Fluency becomes not just possible, but inevitable.

* * *

Thriving Thinking Questions

- What small, consistent actions can I commit to today that will move me closer to becoming more interculturally fluent?
- How does clarifying my "why" give me strength and motivation to stay committed when challenges arise?
- Which practices will help me track my progress and celebrate growth, rather than waiting for a "perfect" milestone?
- How will I intentionally engage in the Learn–Adapt–Immerse–Reflect cycle as a lifelong rhythm for intercultural growth?

15

Final Reflection

Congratulations!

You have taken a significant step in your Intercultural Fluency development. You have already begun the journey toward cultural fluency by engaging with these ideas, reflecting on your experiences, and exploring new ways of seeing and being. This journey often asks us to sit with discomfort, examine deeply held assumptions, and practice humility.

This work is not always easy. Yet it is in these very moments that growth becomes possible. Thank you for choosing to grow, to improve, and connect better across cultures.

Remember, this is not an ending but a beginning. The chapters you have completed now serve as the foundation for your continued Intercultural Fluency development.

My hope is that you will carry this learning forward—not just as knowledge, but as action. Every small step can ripple outward, building bridges where barriers once existed—creating more connection, understanding, and equity in the spaces you influence.

Thank you for allowing me the honor of walking with you in this part of your journey. It has been a privilege to play a small role in your development, and I am grateful for your commitment to becoming a more culturally fluent leader, colleague, and neighbor. Your work ahead matters not only for your own growth, but for the more connected world we are creating together.

Remember, every interaction, no matter how small, is an opportunity to practice and embody Intercultural Fluency.

Happy thriving across cultures!

Thriving Thinking: Final Reflections

As you close this book, pause to reflect on the journey you've taken. You have explored culture, Intercultural Fluency, the four pillars of CQ, subdimensions, and the developmental model. You've learned strategies for applying CQ both professionally and personally. These final reflection questions invite you to integrate your insights, identify actionable next steps, and set intentions for continued growth. Feel free to return to these questions over time, as your understanding deepens and your intercultural practice evolves.

Insights and Lessons

Reflect on what you have learned about yourself, others, and Intercultural Fluency. These questions help you identify key takeaways and patterns:

1. Looking back over all the chapters, what are the three most important insights or lessons you have gained about yourself, culture, and Intercultural Fluency? How do these lessons connect and inform each other?

2. Think of a recent intercultural interaction that went well or could have gone better. How would you approach it differently now, using the frameworks and strategies from this book? What did the experience teach you about yourself and others?

3. Identify any biases, assumptions, or habits that may limit your intercultural effectiveness. How can you consciously counteract them while maintaining authenticity and respect for other cultures?

Action and Application

These questions focus on translating learning into practical steps you can take in your daily life:

1. How can you apply the principles of Intercultural Fluency in your everyday life: at work, at home, and in your community? Identify at least two concrete actions you will take in the next month.

2. Review the subdimensions of CQ (planning, awareness, checking, cultural knowledge, intrinsic/extrinsic motivation, self-efficacy, verbal and nonverbal behaviors). Which subdimensions do you want to target for focused growth? What specific steps can you take to make these skills habitual?

3. Imagine yourself one year from now, practicing Intercultural Fluency intentionally. What would success look like in your relationships, work, and community interactions? How will you measure your progress, and what resources or practices will support you along the way?

Motivation and Growth

These questions help you explore your ongoing commitment, motivation, and areas for intentional focus:

1. Reflect on your motivation to continue developing Intercultural Fluency. What excites you about ongoing growth, and what challenges might you face? How can you sustain curiosity, openness, and resilience in the face of discomfort or setbacks?
2. Consider each pillar of Cultural Intelligence (metacognitive, cognitive, motivational, and behavioral). Which pillar feels most developed in your life, and which requires intentional focus? How will you strengthen the less-developed pillars moving forward?
3. What is your personal commitment to ongoing intercultural growth? Write a short statement or mantra that reminds you of your purpose, motivates action, and inspires reflection whenever you face new cultural experiences.

Supporting Others

These questions invite you to consider your role in fostering Intercultural Fluency beyond yourself:

1. How can you encourage and support others in developing Intercultural Fluency? What role might you play as a mentor, collaborator, or advocate for cultural understanding in your environment?

Ready to Take Your Intercultural Fluency to the Next Level?

Accountability is a fundamental part of the development process. The complex and dynamic nature of culture can make the process feel daunting and overwhelming, which can lead to feeling stuck in development. If you find yourself in this place, you are not alone, and do not give up.

It would be my honor to partner with you in your Intercultural Fluency Development either through Individualized Intercultural Coaching or in one of my Intercultural Fluency Program Pathways that dive even deeper into the Intercultural Fluency Developmental Model and provide you with resources and tools to accelerate your development.

Feel free to visit www.eprocoaching.com for more information or contact me directly using the information provided in the Author Bio Section of this book.

Additional Resources

Intercultural Fluency Program Pathways

EPC Self-Assessments & Resources

EPC Coaching Services

EPC Consulting Services

Substack Newsletter:
www.eprocoaching.
substack.com

YouTube:
www.youtube.com/
eprocoaching

Author Bio

Dr. Jennifer L. Figueroa is a leadership coach and consultant, Intercultural Fluency expert, and strategic thinker dedicated to helping individuals and organizations thrive in a diverse and interconnected world. She holds a doctorate in Strategic Leadership with a concentration in Leadership Coaching, combining deep academic expertise with extensive coaching experience to guide clients through meaningful personal and professional transformation.

As the founder of Eudaimonia Professional Coaching, Dr. Figueroa helps leaders cultivate Intercultural Fluency through cultural intelligence, awareness, and adaptive communication skills that foster authentic connection across cultures. She designs hybrid learning experiences, reflective practices, and customized coaching programs that inspire growth, resilience, and high-impact leadership.

A devoted follower of Christ, Dr. Figueroa integrates authenticity, compassion, and spiritual depth into every facet of her work. Through writing, teaching, and speaking, she encourages others to embrace cultural diversity as a source of strength, creativity, and global influence.

To learn more about her coaching programs, workshops, or speaking engagements, or to connect with Dr. Figueroa for guidance on thriving across cultures, visit or follow her on the platforms listed on the following page.

Let's Connect

Visit our website:
www.eprocoaching.com

LinkedIn:
www.linkedin.com/drfig

Instagram:
@eudaimonia.coaching

Facebook:
www.facebook.com/
eprocoaching/

Connect with Dr. Figueroa & Eudaimonia Professional Coaching

Glossary of Terms

- **_Adapt Stage_** – Stage of the Intercultural Fluency Developmental Model that refers to the part of the process in which one applies and adapts the acquired knowledge from the "Learn" stage to build cultural awareness, as well as adapt one's methodology for navigation of intercultural interactions and cultural differences.
- **_Adaptation_** - "to make fit (as for a new use) often by modification" (Merriam-Webster, n.d.).
- **_Adopt_** - "to begin to practice or use" (Merriam-Webster, n.d.).
- **_Artifacts and Products_** – Something produced or created within a culture.
- **_Assimilate_** - "to absorb into the cultural tradition of a population or group" or "to make similar" (Merriam-Webster, n.d.).
- **_Beliefs/Assumptions_** - core beliefs or assumptions about universal elements across cultures that influence behavior or understanding (ex: time).
- **_Behaviors_** – how one culturally acts, behaves, or conducts oneself.
- **_Cultural Intelligence_** - "A multidimensional framework of the capability to effectively function in culturally diverse contexts" (Figueroa, 2025).
- **_Culture_** – a collection of internal and external parameters (including norms, values, beliefs, assumptions, behaviors, language, motiva-

tions, identities, interpretations of meaning and significant events) resulting from common experiences shared by a distinct group across age generations which distinguishes its members from other groups.

· ***Essential Plurality*** – the idea that culture is essentially plural.

· ***Ethnocentric*** - Assumes one's own culture is central to reality (Rosinski, 2003, p. 31).

· ***Ethnorelative*** - Perceives cultural differences as inevitable without assuming the centrality of one's own culture (Rosinski, 2003, p. 34).

· ***Globalization*** - "The action, process, or fact of making global; *esp.* (in later use) the process by which businesses or other organizations develop international influence or start operating on an international scale" (Oxford English Dictionary, n.d.).

· ***Immerse Stage*** - Stage of the Intercultural Fluency Developmental Model that refers to the intercultural interaction as the practicing and expression of the knowledge gained, adaptations formed, and awareness realized in the previous "Learn" and "Adapt" stages.

· ***Intelligence*** - "The ability to learn or understand or to deal with new or trying situations" or "the act of understanding" (Merriam-Webster, n.d.). Or "the ability to solve problems and to create a product in several ways" (Gardener, 1983; Yavich & Rotnitsky, 2020, p. 108).

· ***Intercultural Fluency*** - Having or showing mastery of both perceptions and interactions occurring between two or more cultures, capable of communicating easily and accurately between two or more cultures, or engaging two or more cultures effectively and successfully (Figueroa, 2024).

· ***Intercultural Fluency Developmental Model*** – a model that represents the stages, progression, and components of Intercultural Fluency Development.

· ***Language*** – "the words, their pronunciation, and the methods of

125

combining them used and understood by a community" (Merriam-Webster, n.d.).

- *Learn Stage* – Stage of the Intercultural Fluency Developmental Model that refers to the acquisition of cultural knowledge and information (general and context specific).
- *Motivation* – Central component in the Intercultural Fluency Developmental Model. Refers to one's motivation to continually engage with each stage of the process.
- *Multidimensional Framework of Intelligence* - "Concept of intelligence not being singular but multifaceted containing several different capabilities to understand intelligence organized by type: metacognition, cognition, motivational, and behavioral (Van Dyne et al., 2012, p. 297; Sternberg & Detterman, 1986).
- *Multiple Loci of Intelligence Framework* – "One's intelligence derived from multiple interrelated sources within the person (Van Dyne et al., 2012, p. 297; Sternberg, 1986).
- *Norms* – "What is considered right, appropriate, and acceptable by the cultural group" (Rosinski, 2003, p. 24).
- *Reflect Stage* – Stage of the Intercultural Fluency Developmental Model that refers to the part of the process in which one sets aside time after the intercultural interaction to thoughtfully engage in reflective evaluation of one's navigation of cultural differences and employment of intercultural skills.
- *Symbols* – a culturally specific visible sign or image.
- *Theory of Multiple Intelligences* – A concept of multiple types of intelligence highlighting "different and autonomous intelligence capacities that result in many different ways of knowing, understanding, and learning about the world to have a better understanding of it" (Gardener, 1993; Razmjoo, 2008, p. 155).
- *Values* – "Ideals shared by the [cultural] group" (Rosinski, 2003, p. 24).

References

A

Ailon, G. (2008). Mirror, mirror on the wall: *Culture's Consequences* in a value test of its own design. *Academy of Management Review, 33,* 885–904.

Ang, S., Van Dyne, L., Koh, C., Ng, K. Y., Templer, K. J., Tay, C., & Chandrasekar, N. A. (2007). Cultural intelligence: Its measurement and effects on cultural judgment and decision making, cultural adaptation, and task performance. *Management and Organization Review, 3*(3), 335–371.

Ang, S., & Van Dyne, L. (Eds.). (2008). *Handbook of cultural intelligence: Theory, measurement, and applications.* New York, NY: Routledge.

B

Bandura, A. (1997). *Self-Efficacy: The Exercise of Control.* New York: Freeman.

Bandura, A. (2002). Social cognitive theory in a cultural context. *Applied Psychology: An International Review,* 51, 269-290.

Baran, B. E., & Woznyj, H. M. (2021). Managing VUCA: The human dynamics of agility. *Organizational Dynamics,* 50(1), 100787. https://doi.org/10.1016/j.orgdyn.2020.100787

Bartel-Radic, A. (2013). "Estrangeirismo" and flexibility: intercultural learning in Brazilian MNCs. *International Management*, 17(4), 239–253.

Barzantny, C. (2013, September). Review of *Global Leadership: Research, Practice, and Development (Book)*. *Academy of Management Learning & Education*, 12(3), 530–532.

Beamer, L., & Varner, I. (2001). Intercultural Communication in the Global Workplace. Boston: McGraw-Hill.

Bell, B. S., & Kozlowski, S. W. J. (2008). Active learning: Effects of core training design elements on self-regulatory processes, learning, and adaptability. *Journal of Applied Psychology*, 93, 296-316.

Bennett, M. J. (1993). Towards ethno-relativism: A developmental model of cultural sensitivity, in *Education for the Intercultural Experience*, ed RM Paige, pp 21-71, Intercultural Press, Yarmouth.

Bennett, J. M. (2007, March). *Curiosity: The key to intercultural competence.* Paper presented at the Families in Global Transition (FIGT) Conference, Houston, TX.

Bordei, S. (2017). How can one possibly determine the multiple intelligences? Journal Plus Education, 18(2), 204-212. https://doi.org/10.24250/jpe/2/2017/SB

Bowe, H.J., & Martin, K. (2007). *Communication Across Cultures: Mutual Understanding in a Global World.* Cambridge: Cambridge University Press.

Brislin, R., Worthle, R., MacNab, B. (2006). *Cultural intelligence: understanding behaviors that serve people's goals.* Group Org. Manag. 31, 40-55.

Bubic, A., von Cramon, D., & Schubotz, R. I. (2010). Prediction, cognition and the brain. *Frontiers in Human Neuroscience*, 4, 1–15.

Buchynska, M. (2022, November 21). *4 things all great listeners know.* YouTube. https://www.youtube.com/watch?v=i3ku5nx4tMU

Business School 101. (2021, April 22). *Hofstede Cultural Framework | International Business| From A Business Professor#Hofstede.* YouTube. https://www.youtube.com/watch?v=TXofUAhBAfc

C

Campbell, B. (1992). Multiple intelligences in action. *Childhood Education*, 68(4), 197–200. https://www.tandfonline.com/doi/pdf/10.1080/00094056.1992.10520874

Chhokar, J. S., Brodbeck, F. C., & House, R. J. (2019). *Culture and leadership across the world the Globe Book of in-depth studies of 25 societies.* Psychology Press.

Clegg, K., Houston, G., & Gower, O. (2024). *Doctoral Supervision and Research Culture: What we know, what works and why* (1st ed.). Routledge.

Cosman, O. (2021). Cultural Differences in Business Communication. *The USV Annals of Economics and Public Administration*, 21(1), 78–87.

Couch, S., & Rose, S. (2020). Coaching culturally different members of international business teams – the role of Cultural Intelligence. *International Coaching Psychology Review*, 15(1), 59–80. https://doi.org/10.53841/bpsicpr.2020.15.1.59

Cox, E., Bachkirova, T., & Clutterbuck, D. (2024). *The Complete Handbook of Coaching* (4th ed.). SAGE.

Crowne, K. A. (2009). The relationships among social intelligence, emotional intelligence, and cultural intelligence. *Organization Management Journal*, 6(3), 148–163. https://scholarship.shu.edu/cgi/viewcontent.cgi?article=1189&context=omj

Cultures and Organizations, Software of the Mind (2010). Scores of the Arabic States are based on Almutairi, S., Heller, M., & Yen, D. (2020). Reclaiming the heterogeneity of the Arab states. Cross Cultural & Strategic Management.

Curran, R., Ripolles, M., Musteen, M., Blesa, A., & Arroteia, N. (2021). Improving Cultural Intelligence, Psychological Empowerment, and Task Performance in the Classroom: Global Game Challenge. *JOURNAL OF TEACHING IN INTERNATIONAL BUSINESS*, 32(1), 36–56.

D

Deci, E. L. (1975). *Intrinsic Motivation.* New York: Plenum Press.

E

Earley, P. C., & Ang, S. (2003). *Cultural intelligence: Individual interactions across cultures.* Palo Alto, CA: Stanford University Press.

Eccles, J. S., & Wigfield, A. (2002). Motivational beliefs, values, and goals. In S. T. Fiske, D. L. Schacter & C. Zahn-Waxler (Eds.), *Annual Review of Psychology*, Vol. 53. (pp. 109-132). Palo Alto, CA: Annual Reviews.

Endsley, M. R. (1995). Toward a theory of situation awareness in dynamic systems. Human Factors, 37, 32–64.

English, S., Sabatine, J. M., & Brownell, P. (2019). *Professional coaching: Principles and practice.* Springer Publishing Company, LLC.

F

Figueroa, J. (2025). *Intercultural Fluency Program* [Doctoral project, Oral Roberts University].

Flavell, J. H. (1979). Meta-cognition and cognitive monitoring: A new area of cognitive inquiry. *American Psychologist*, 34, 906-911.

Franklin, L. (2017, December 19). Reading minds through body language | Lynne Franklin | TEDxNaperville. YouTube. https://www.youtube.com/watch?v=W3P3rToj2gQ

G

Gallo, A., Gidal, J., & LaPierre, S. (2022, August 31). The Art of Active Listening | The Harvard Business Review Guide. YouTube. https://www.youtube.com/watch?v=aDMtx5ivKK0

Gardner, H. (1983). Frames of mind: The theory of multiple intelligences. U.S.A: Basic Books.

Gardner, H. (1993). Multiple intelligences: The theory in practice. New York: Basic books.

Gardner, H. (1999). Intelligence reframed. New York: Basic Books.

Gouws, F. E. (2007). Teaching and Learning Through Multiple intelligences in the Outcomes-based Education Classroom . Africa Education Review, 4(2), 60-74. https://doi.org/10.1080/1814662070 1652705

Gregerson, H., Morrison, A. J., & Black, J. S. (1998). Developing leaders for the global frontier. Sloan Management Review, 40(1), 21-32. Retrieved from http://sloanreview.mit.edu/article/developing-leaders-for-the-global-frontier/

Gudykunst, W. B., & Kim, Y. Y. (1984). Communicating with Strangers. Beverly Hills, CA: Sage.

Gupta, A.K & Govindarajan, V. (2002). Cultivating a global mindset. Academy of Management Executive, 16(1), 116-126.

H

Hall, ET. (1989). Beyond Culture, Anchor House, New York.

Harvard Business Review. (2022, August 31). The art of active listening | The Harvard Business Review Guide. YouTube. https://www.youtube.com/watch?v=aDMtx5ivKK0

Helpful Professor Explains! (2024, July 4). Cultural Dimensions Theory (Explained in 3 Minutes). YouTube. https://www.youtube.com/watch?v=

bac1wWSgQMs

Hett, E.J. (1993). The Development of an Instrument to Measure Global-Mindedness. *Doctoral Thesis, University of San Diego*

Hofstede, G. (1980a). *Culture's consequences: International differences in work-related values.* Beverly Hills, CA: Sage.

Hofstede, G. (1980b). Motivation, leadership, and organization: Do American theories apply abroad? Organizational Dynamics, 9, 42–63.

Hofstede, G. (1984). Culture's Consequences, Sage Publications.

Hofstede, G. (1991). Cultures and Organizations: Software of the Mind: Intercultural Cooperation and Its Importance for Survival, McGraw-Hill Publishing Co.

Hofstede, G. (1993). Cultural Constraints in Management Theories. *The Executive*, 7(1), 81–94. http://www.jstor.org/stable/4165110

Hofstede, G. (1994). Management scientists are human. Management Science, 40, 4–14.

Hofstede, G. (2001). Culture's consequences: Comparing values, behav- iors, institutions, and organizations across nations (2nd ed.). London, England: Sage.

Hofstede, G. (n.d.). *National culture.* Hofstede insights. Retrieved from https://hi.hofstede-insights.com/national-culture

Hofstede, G. (2011). Dimensionalizing Cultures: The Hofstede Model in Context. *Online Readings in Psychology and Culture.*

Home: Oxford English Dictionary. OED: Oxford English Dictionary. (n.d.). https://www.oed.com/

House, R. J., Javidan, M., Hanges, P., & Dorfman, P. (2002). Under- standing cultures and implicit leadership theories across the globe: An introduction to project GLOBE. Journal of World Business, 37: 3–10.

House, R. J., Hanges, P. J., Javidan, M., Dorfman, P. W., & Gupta, V. (Eds.). (2004). *Culture, leadership, and organizations: The Globe Study of 62 societies* (1st ed.). Sage Publications, Inc.

Hruby, J. (2023, May 4). *What does it mean to have a GLOBAL MINDSET.*

YouTube. https://www.youtube.com/watch?v=tZTS8fLmAr8

Hunter, B., White, G.O. & Godbey, G.C. (2006). What does it mean to be globally competent? *Journal of Studies in International Education*, 10, 267-286.

I

Intercultural Development Inventory. (n.d.). *Intercultural Development Continuum (IDC)*. Retrieved February 23, 2025, from https://www.idiinventory.com/idc

J

Jacobs, J.E., & Paris, S. G. (1987). Children's metacognition about reading: Issues in definition, measurement, and instruction. *Educational Psychologist*, 22, 143-158.

Jain, C., & Choudhary, M. (2011). *Actions speak louder than words: Nonverbal mis/communication. Journal of Media and Communication Studies*, 3(5), 121–128. Retrieved from https://academicjournals.org/article/article1380104425_Jain%20and%20Choudhary.pdf

Javidan, M., Dorfman, P. W., Sully de Luque, M., & House, R. J. (2006). In the Eye of the Beholder: Cross Cultural Lessons in Leadership from Project GLOBE. *Academy of Management Perspectives*, 20(1), 67–90. http://www.jstor.org/stable/4166219

Javidan, M., Teagarden, M., Babrinde, F., Walch, K., Lynton, N., Pearson, D., Bowen, D. & Cabrera, A. (2011) Global Mindset Defined: Expat success strategy. *Worldwide ERC Foundation*. Retrieved 10th January 2011 from http://www.worldwideerc.org/Foundation/Documents/global_mindset.pdf

K

Kanfer, R. (forthcoming). Work motivation: Theory, practice, and future directions. In S. W. J. Kozlowski (Ed.), *The Oxford Handbook of Industrial and Organizational Psychology*. New York: Oxford University Press.

Keith, N., & Frese, M. (2005). Self-regulation in error management training: Emotion control and metacognition as mediators of performance effects. *Journal of Applied Psychology, 90,* 677–691.

Keung, E. K. (2011). *What factors of cultural intelligence predict transformational leadership: A Study of International School leaders* (dissertation). *What Factors of Cultural Intelligence Predict Transformational Leadership: a Study of International School Leaders.* Liberty University, Lynchburg, Va.

Knapp, M., & Hall, J. (2010). *Nonverbal Communication in Human Interaction* (7th ed). Boston, MA: Wadsworth.

Küry, L., & Fischer, C. (2025). *The self-perceptions of twice-exceptional children: A systematic review. Education Sciences, 15*(1), 44. https://doi.org/10.3390/educsci15010044

L

Le, E. T. (2016). *Evaluating The Predictive Validity of The Global Competencies Inventory For Determining Global Leadership Outcomes* (dissertation). ProQuest LLC, Ann Arbor, MI.

Locken, F. (2024, March 13). *Cultural Intelligence – Bridging the Gap Between Cultures | Faith Locken | TEDxAlleyns School Youth.* YouTube. https://www.youtube.com/watch?v=vbQHxjZyKHs

Lokkesmoe, K. J. (2009). *A Grounded Theory Study Of Effective Global Leadership Development Strategies: Perspectives From Brazil, India, And Nigeria* (dissertation). ProQuest LLC, Ann Arbor, MI.

Lundvall, S. (2015). *Physical literacy in the field of physical education–A challenge and a possibility. Journal of Sport and Health Science, 4*(3), 1–8.

https://www.sciencedirect.com/science/article/pii/S2095254615000228

M

Manzoor, Q. A. (2012). *Impact of employee motivation on organizational effectiveness. Business Management and Strategy, 3*(1), 1–12. https://www.academia.edu/download/36733445/150.pdf

Mendenhall, M. E., Osland, J. S., Bird, A., Oddou, G., Stevens, M. J., Maznevski, M. L., & Stahl, G. K. (2018). *Global leadership: Research, practice, and development* (3rd ed.). Routledge.

Mendenhall, M. E., Arnardottir, A. A., Oddou, G. R., & Burke, L. A. (2013). Developing Cross-Cultural Competencies in Management Education via Cognitive-Behavior Therapy. *Academy of Management Learning & Education, 12*(3), 436–451.

Merriam-Webster. (n.d.). *America's most trusted dictionary.* Merriam-Webster. https://www.merriam-webster.com/

Minkov, M., & Kaasa, A. (2022). Do dimensions of culture exist objectively? A validation of the revised Minkov-Hofstede model of culture with World Values Survey items and scores for 102 countries. Journal of International Management, 28(4), 100971.

Munley, A. E. (2011). Culture Differences in Leadership. *The IUP Journal of Soft Skills, V*(1), 16–30.

Mutlu, C., & Arıkboğa, F. Ş. (2024). *The mediating role of cultural intelligence in the relationship between personality and cross-cultural adaptability: A research on graduate students.* Doğuş University Journal, 25(2), 315–334. https://doi.org/10.31671/doujournal.1343316

N

Nagdaseva, O. (2018, May 29). *The Power of the Global Mind | Olga Nagdaseva | TEDxAkron.* YouTube. https://www.youtube.com/watch?v=dx5trxiPSm8

Norcross JC, Ratzin AC, Payne D. Ringing in the new year: The change processes and reported outcomes of resolutions. Addict Behav. 1989;14(2):205–212. pmid:2728957

O

Oscarsson, M., Carlbring, P., Andersson, G., & Rozental, A. (2020). *A large-scale experiment on New Year's resolutions: Approach-oriented goals are more successful than avoidance-oriented goals.* PLOS ONE, 15(12), e0234097. https://doi.org/10.1371/journal.pone.0234097

P

Palmer, S., & Whybrow, A. (2019). *Handbook of Coaching Psychology a guide for Practitioners* (2nd ed.). Routledge.

Passmore, J. (2021). *Excellence in coaching: Theory, tools and techniques to achieve outstanding coaching performance* (4th ed.). Kogan Page.

Pellegrino, L. (1982). *Nonverbal communication and its implications for therapeutic recreation practitioners working with severely-profoundly handicapped individuals.* ScholarWorks at California State University. Retrieved from https://scholarworks.calstate.edu/downloads/vh53wz798

Perez, J. R. (2017). Global leadership and the impact of globalization. *Journal of Leadership, Accountability and Ethics,* 14(3), 48-52.

Perlmutter, H. (1969) The tortuous evolution of the multinational corporation, *Columbia Journal of World Business,* 1(1), pp. 9-18.

Plaister-Ten, J. (2013). Raising culturally-derived awareness and building culturally-appropriate responsibility: The development of the Cross-Cultural Kaleidoscope. *International Journal of Evidence Based Coaching and Mentoring*, 11(2), 52–69.

R

Razmjoo, S. A. (2008). On the relationship between multiple intelligences and language proficiency. *The Reading Matrix*, 8(2), 155–164. https://www.readingmatrix.com/articles/razmjoo/article.pdf

Rhinesmith, S.H. (1992) Global mindsets for global managers, *Training and Development*, 46(10) pp. 63-69.

Ridley, D. S., Schutz, P. A., Glanz, R. S., & Weinstein, C. E. (1992). Self-regulated learning: The interactive influence of metacognitive awareness and goal-setting. *Journal of Experimental Education*, 60, 293-306.

Rosinski, P. (1999). *Beyond Intercultural Sensitivity: Leveraging Cultural Differences.*

Rosinski, P. (2003). *Coaching across cultures: New Tools for Leveraging National, corporate and professional differences.* Nicholas Brealey Publishing.

Rosinski, P. (2010). *Global coaching: An integrated approach for long-lasting results.* Nicholas Brealey Pub.

Ryan, R. M. & Deci, E. L. (2000). Intrinsic and extrinsic motivations: Classic definitions and new directions. *Contemporary Educational Psychology*, 25, 54-67.

S

Schmidt, A. M., & Ford, J. K. (2003). Learning within a learner control training environment: The interactive effects of goal orientation and metacognitive instruction on learning outcomes. Personnel Psychology, 56, 405– 429.

Schwartz, S.H. (2009). Culture matters: National value cultures, sources and consequences. In R.S. Wyer, Cy. Chiu, & Y.y. Hong (Eds.), *Understanding Culture: Theory, research and application* (pp. 127-150). London: Psychology Press.

Sheridan, E. (2005). *Intercultural Leadership Competencies For U.S. Business Leaders In The New Millennium* (dissertation). ProQuest Learning and Information Company, Ann Arbor, MI.

Sirakaya, Y. (2025). *Conceptual evaluation of the impact of the link between remote working and work-life balance on employee motivation. IRASS Journal of Multidisciplinary Studies,* 2(1), 1–9. Retrieved from https://irasspublisher.com/assets/articles/1736068578.pdf

Sivers, D. (2010, January 29). *Weird, or just different? | Derek Sivers.* YouTube. https://www.youtube.com/watch?v=1K5SycZjGhI

Skaria, R., & Montayre, J. (2023). *Cultural intelligence and intercultural effectiveness among nurse educators: A mixed-method study.* Nurse Education Today, 121, 105714. https://doi.org/10.1016/j.nedt.2023.10 5714

Spitzberg, B., & Changnon, G. (2009). Conceptualizing intercultural competence. In D. K. Deardorff (Ed.), *The Sage handbook of intercultural competence* (pp. 2-52). Thousand Oaks, CA: Sage.

Sternberg, R. J., & Detterman, D. K. (Eds.). (1986). *What is intelligence? Contemporary viewpoints on its nature and definition.* Norwood, NJ: Ablex Publishing.

T

Taras, V., Kirkman, B. L., & Steel, P. (2010). Examining the Impact of Culture's Consequences: A Three-Decade, Multilevel, Meta-Analytic Review of Hofstede's Cultural Value Dimensions. *Journal of Applied Psychology*, 95(3), 405–439.

Texas A&M Mays Business School. (2017, December 21). *What is a Global Mindset?*. YouTube. https://www.youtube.com/watch?v=6nr-rj4EzhM

Thomas, J. (2014, December 8). *Cultural intelligence — a new way to think about global effectiveness | Jeff Thomas | TEDxSpokane*. YouTube. https://www.youtube.com/watch?v=K3S76gAKp6Q

Triandis, H.C. (2006). Cultural Intelligence in Organizations. Group and Organization Management, 31, 20-26.

Tucker, M. F., Bonial, R., Vanhove, A., & Kedharnath, U. (2014). Leading across cultures in the human age: An empirical investigation of intercultural competency among global leaders. *SpringerPlus, 3*, 127. https://doi.org/10.1186/2193-1801-3-127

V

Van Dyne, L., Ang, S., Yee Ng, K., Rockstuhl, T., Ling Tan, M., & Koh, C. (2012). Sub-Dimensions of the Four Factor Model of Cultural Intelligence: Expanding the Conceptualization and Measurement of Cultural Intelligence. *Social and Personality Psychology Compass, 6(4)*, 295–313.

Van Luinen, E. (2016). *Global Leadership: Strategies And Practices To Develop Intercultural Skills* (dissertation). ProQuest LLC, Ann Arbor, MI.

Victor, D. (1992). International Business Communication. New York: HarperCollins.

W

Wang, H., Waldman, D. A., & Zhang, H. (2012). Strategic leadership across cultures: Current findings and future research directions. *Journal of World Business*, 47(4), 571–580. https://doi.org/10.1016/j.jwb.2012.01.010

Westphal, M., Seivert, N. H., & Bonanno, G. A. (2010). Expressive flexibility. *Emotion*, 10, 92–100.

Whitmore, J. (2017). *Coaching for performance: The principles and practice of coaching and leadership* (5th ed.). Nicholas Brealey Publishing.

Wilson, W. (2013). Coaching with a Global Mindset. *International Journal of Evidence Based Coaching and Mentoring*, 11(2), 33–52.

Williams, P., & Menendez, D. S. (2023). *Becoming a professional life coach: The Art and Science of a whole-person approach* (3rd ed.). Norton Professional Books.

Willis-Shattuck, M., Bidwell, P., & Thomas, S. (2008). *Motivation and retention of health workers in developing countries: A systematic review*. BMC Health Services Research, 8(247), 1–10. *https://link.springer.com/article/10.1186/1472-6963-8-247*

Y

Yavich, R., & Rotnitsky, I. (2020). Multiple intelligences and success in school studies. *International Journal of Higher Education*, 9(3), 191–201. https://files.eric.ed.gov/fulltext/EJ1277917.pdf

Ylänne, V. (2008). Communication accommodation theory. In H. Spencer-Oatey (Ed.), *Culturally Speaking: Culture, Communication, and Politeness Theory* (2nd ed pp. 164–186). London: Continuum.

Yousef, K. (2020). *Four pillars of cross-cultural management: A systematic literature review*. Budapest Management Review, 51(5). https://doi.org/10.14267/veztud.2020.05.03

Z

Zhong, J. Y. (2024). *Investigating intrinsic motivation for learning among Singaporean youths: A mixed methods study.* SSRN. Retrieved from https://download.ssrn.com

Appendix

Figure 3.1 & 3.2

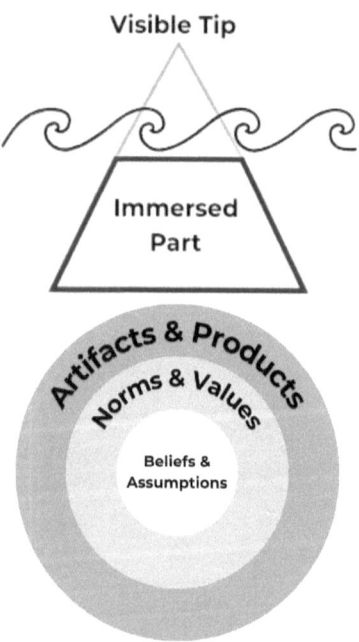

Figure 3.1 & Figure 3.2 – Iceberg Model (adapted from Rosinski, 2003) & Onion Model (adapted from Rosinski, 2003).

Figure 9.1 & 10.1

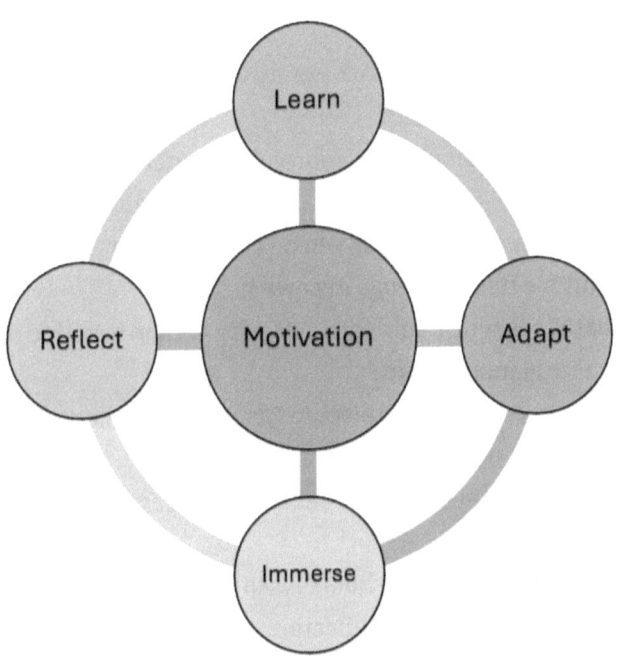

Figure 9.1 & 10.1 The Intercultural Fluency Developmental Model (Figueroa, 2025).

Commitment Contract Guiding Questions

If you are unsure where to start, feel free to use the following questions to guide you:

- What does "showing up with honesty" mean to me in the context of intercultural growth?
- How will I remind myself to embrace discomfort instead of avoiding it?
- How can I practice openness when I encounter perspectives, values, or traditions that challenge my own?
- In what ways will I cultivate curiosity rather than judgment in intercultural interactions?
- What practices will I put in place to ensure I honor the confidentiality and dignity of others' stories?
- How do I want others to feel when they engage with me in culturally diverse contexts?
- What actions can I take to hold myself accountable for my intercultural growth (journaling, reflection, feedback, etc.)?
- How will I balance my personal development with applying these skills in professional and leadership settings?
- Who can I invite into my journey to provide honest feedback about how I show up across cultures?
- How will I keep my learning active beyond this book so that intercultural fluency becomes a lifelong practice?
- In what ways can I use my role, platform, or influence to foster inclusion, equity, and belonging in my circles of impact?
- What commitments can I make to being a bridge-builder, especially in moments of tension or misunderstanding?
- How will I integrate intercultural fluency practices into my daily life (work, relationships, community)?

- What personal values or faith convictions inspire me to live out these commitments with integrity?
- What kind of intercultural practitioner do I want to be remembered as by those I work and live with?
- How will I carry forward the mindset that intercultural fluency is not a one-time achievement but a lifelong journey?

Reflect Stage Guiding Questions

In the reflect stage, you will think back on the interaction, using guiding questions to reflect and evaluate your intercultural effectiveness. You may use the following guiding questions as a starting point:

- What did I notice throughout the interaction?
- Were there behaviors, information, or adaptations that resonated well during the interaction?
- Were there behaviors, information, or adaptations that resonated poorly during the interaction?
- What feedback did I or can I get from those in the interaction?
- What feedback did I or can I get from those who observed the interaction?
- Was the information I acquired accurate? Was it inaccurate?
- How comfortable did I feel? How comfortable were the others in the interaction?
- How can I do better next time?
- What information, adaptations, or behaviors were missing in this interaction?
- In what ways do I need to acquire more information or better apply/adapt the information I have so that I can improve the next interaction?